Japanese Gardens

Japan

ese Gardens Design and Meaning

Mitchell Bring

Josse Wayembergh

McGraw-Hill Book Company

New York St. Louis San Francisco Auckland
Bogotá Hamburg Johannesburg London
Madrid Mexico Montreal New Delhi
Panama São Paulo Singapore
Sydney Tokyo Toronto

McGraw-Hill Series in
LANDSCAPE AND LANDSCAPE ARCHITECTURE

Albert Fein, Ph.D., A.S.L.A.(hon.) *Consulting Editor*

Bring and Wayembergh ■ Japanese Gardens: Design and Meaning
Gold ■ Recreation Planning and Design
Hudak ■ Trees for Every Purpose
Landscape Architecture Magazine ■ Landscapes for Living
Landscape Architecture Magazine ■ Water and the Landscape
Simonds ■ Earthscape

Library of Congress Cataloging in Publication Data

Bring, Mitchell.
  Japanese gardens.

  (McGraw-Hill series in landscape and landscape
architecture)
  Bibliography: p.
  Includes index.
  1. Gardens, Japanese. 2. Gardens—Japan—Kyoto.
I. Wayembergh, Josse, joint author. II. Title.
II. Series.
Sb458.B74   712'.0952   79-27286
ISBN 0-07-007825-4

1234567890   VHVH   8987654321

*The editors for this book were Jeremy Robinson and Esther Gelatt,
the designer was Naomi Auerbach, and the production supervisor
was Sally Fliess. It was set in Optima Medium
by The Clarinda Company.*

Printed and bound by Von Hoffmann Press, Inc.

For my parents
M.B.

For my wife and children
J. W.

Contents

(Continued)

Preface

Study the examples of works left by the past masters and, considering the desires of the owner of the garden, you should create a work of your own by exercising your tasteful sense.
Tachibana Toshitsuna
Sakuteiki, ca. 1100

The purpose of this book is to enable a person unfamiliar with Japanese culture to study some masterworks of Japanese gardening. Each of the ten gardens presented is carefully documented with plans, sections, conceptual drawings, and photographs so that it can be visualized in terms of both overall design and specific details. The need for such a work has existed ever since Josiah Conder first introduced the *Landscape Gardening of Japan* to the Western world in the 1890s, for the *complete* image of the Japanese garden has remained vague at best and grossly distorted at worst. A thorough, clear set of descriptive drawings seems long overdue.

The Kyoto gardens selected for study in Part One are among the finest examples of the art. They span a 300-year history during which garden making matured and they demonstrate all the essential elements of the Japanese garden. Diverse in form, size, and intention, they illustrate a broad range of designs yet are close enough in spirit to demonstrate some general principles.

The old adage about the Japanese garden being in harmony with the environment suggests some important questions about ecological understanding. The Japanese garden is indeed natural-looking when compared with the geometric gardens of Europe, but the tremendous amount of labor needed to maintain one certainly precludes any notions of its being a balanced ecosystem. What, then, did the Japanese think of nature, and what meaning did a "garden" have for the medieval Japanese? Certainly it was more than a simple ornament, for it embodied not only religious traditions but an understanding of the mechanics of the environment as well. These questions of natural science and landscape symbolism are dealt with in Part Two.

General principles of visual and spatial design, along with examples of material usage and special details, are presented in Part Three.

Generally speaking, this book has been prepared with a design professional in mind, and no prior knowledge of Japanese culture is assumed. Graphic traditions and examples are emphasized over literary ones. Everything is rendered in English, with Japanese equivalents provided for the more important terms. Japanese words are transliterated according to a modified Hepburn system of romanization, while the Wade-Giles system is used for Chinese terms. People who specialize in East Asian studies will find both the documentation of the gardens (the most graphically comprehensive descriptions published) and the manner of approach (which includes aspects of East Asian cosmology and geomancy) significant enough to sustain their interest. The general reader, perhaps with the idea of a backyard garden in mind, will find a sourcebook of ideas upon which to draw, as well as some insight into the overall significance of Japanese garden forms.

As this book is the result of mutual effort, we would like to express both individual and joint debts of gratitude. Josse Wayembergh wishes to thank Dr. Makoto Arisawa for his endless help in explaining the cultural aspects of the gardens, with the assistance of Professor Toshizo Sasaki.

Mitchell Bring would like to express his thanks to the many people who helped him in writing the text: Michel Strickman for initial help and encouragement; Shigemaro Shimoyama for assistance with the *Sakuteiki;* Carolyn Wheelwright and Andrew Goble for critical reviews and numerous suggestions; Ronald Herman for reviewing the plant materials chart; and Noelle Burke and Barbara Schulenberg for helping prepare the first draft in Brussels. He especially wants to express heartfelt thanks to Yuichi Hirano, friend and tutor at Kyoto University, for patient help with translations, and to Lisa Berkson for endless hours of assistance with translations and critical preparation of the final manuscript.

Jointly we were fortunate to have had the opportunity to spend over four years in Japan, as graduate researchers at Kyoto University's Department of Architecture, and we gratefully acknowledge the financial support from the Japanese Ministry of Education (Mombusho) that made this work possible. We wish to thank our professors, Tomoya Masuda and Kunio Kato of the Faculty of Engineering, Department of Architecture, Kyoto University, for their support and assistance; the numerous museum officials who opened their collections; and the caretakers of the gardens who let us tread on their small gardens with our big shoes. Also we wish to thank Nobuo Shirasuna for help in identifying plant materials; Kinsaku Nakane, of the Kyoto Japanese Garden Institute, who gave generously of his time and information; and Akemi Takada, whose beautiful *kanjii* grace the chapter titles of Part One. Finally, we want to thank Yoshiko Ohashi, of the Kyoto University Foreign Student Service, for her efforts above and beyond the call of duty in making our lives in Japan a little easier.

Mitchell Bring
Josse Wayembergh

chapter one

Introduction

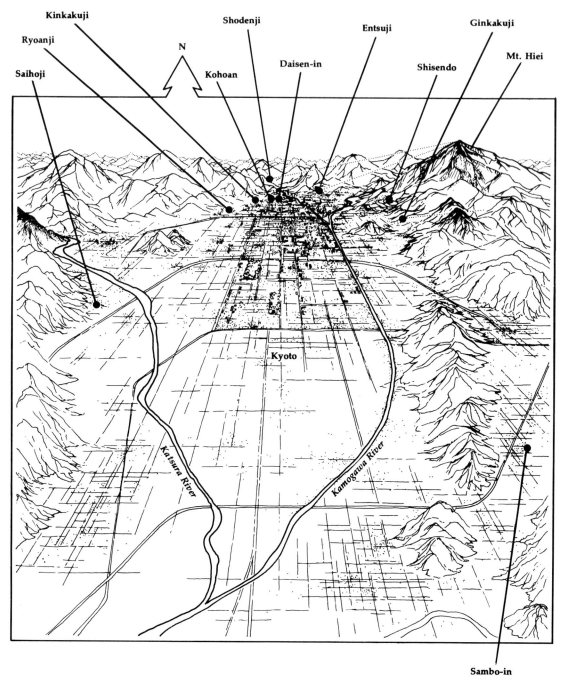

Ryoanji

Saihoji

Kinkakuji

N

Kohoan

Shodenji

Daisen-in

Entsuji

Shisendo

Ginkakuji

Mt. Hiei

Katsura River

Kamogawa River

Kyoto

Sambo-in

fig. 1.1 *Aerial perspective of Kyoto.*

PHYSICAL SETTING

The gardens of this survey are located in Kyoto, where the Japanese garden art reached its zenith. As the home of the Emperor for almost a thousand years, this city served as the setting for many events that shaped political and cultural history. Even today, centuries after the political focus moved to Tokyo, Kyoto remains the seat of traditional culture and stands as a symbol of old Japan.

The city lies on a slightly inclined plane surrounded on three sides by low, rolling mountains (Fig. 1.1). The choice of the site was determined in the eighth century according to the principles of Chinese geomancy—an aesthetic science dealing with the positive management of the landscape in accordance with hidden forces within the earth (Ch. 13). Kyoto's grid plan was a smaller model of the Chinese capital of Ch'ang-an and originally measured 3.5 miles north to south and 3 miles east to west (Figs. 1.2 and 1.3). The north–south axis split the town into symmetrical halves, and at the northern terminus lay the Imperial compound with its buildings arranged according to the hierarchical offices of government. These buildings, like the entire city, all faced southward, the direction the Emperor always faced, toward light and warmth.

fig. 1.2 (left) *Reconstructed plan of Ch'ang-an, the T'ang Dynasty (618–907) Chinese capital that served as the model for Kyoto (redrawn after Boyd).*[1]

fig. 1.3 (right) *Reconstruction of the original plan of Kyoto (redrawn after Itoh).*[2]

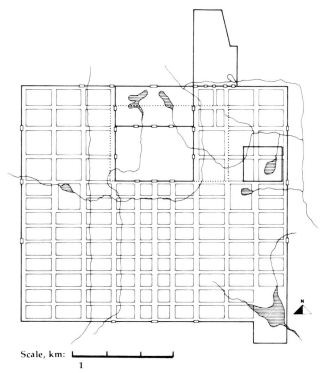

Scale, km: |_____|_____|_____|
1

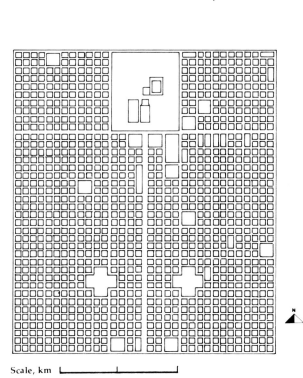

Scale, km |_____|_____|_____|
1

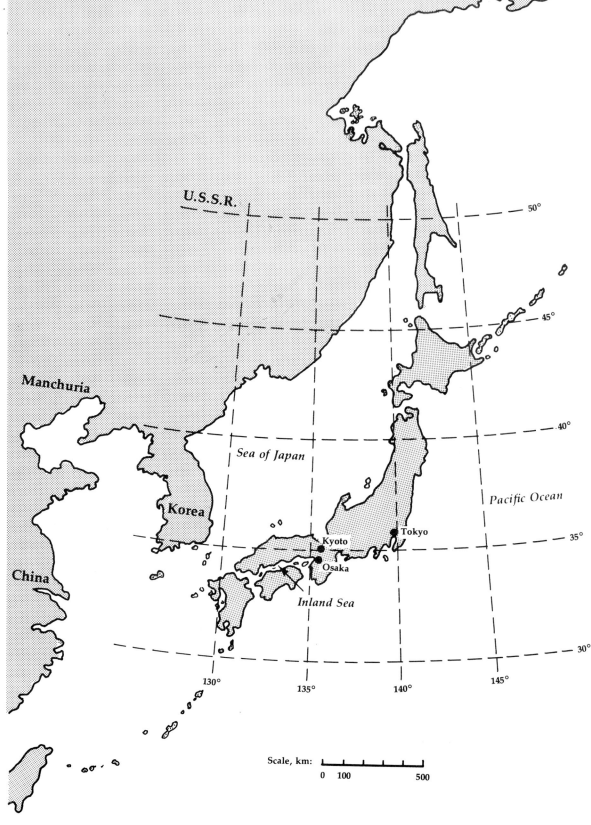

U.S.S.R.

Manchuria

Sea of Japan

Korea

China

Pacific Ocean

Kyoto

Osaka

Tokyo

Inland Sea

50°

45°

40°

35°

30°

130°   135°   140°   145°

Scale, km:

0   100   500

Although Kyoto lies only thirty miles from the Inland Sea, its climate is much less temperate than nearby coastal cities (Fig. 1.4). The surrounding mountains that give Kyoto so much of its physical beauty also have an adverse climatic effect in that they block off the cooling winds during summer, when the humidity is highest, and help retain the damp, penetrating cold during winter (Fig. 1.5). These same hills are the source of the numerous springs and rivers that provide Kyoto with an ample year-long supply of fresh water for garden waterfalls and ponds. Water availability, enhanced by a system of canals built early in the city's history, was especially important in garden making, as the water's cooling effect helped make the Kyoto summer bearable.

The weather is the source of many complaints from the Kyoto residents, but it favors vegetation. Pine and cypress groves carpet the mountains with a lush green color, while moss grows easily and has become a Kyoto garden trademark. Moss proved almost impossible to grow in the reproductions of Kyoto gardens attempted in the drier climate of the later capital, Tokyo.

Figure 1.1 shows the location of the surveyed gardens in Kyoto, revealing that almost all the gardens lie on the outskirts of the city and near the foot of the mountains. This is so for a number of reasons: These suburban sites were considered to be some of the most beautiful; geomantic landscape practice found it particularly fortuitous to build at the base of a mountain; and many of the fine gardens built within the original city plan have been destroyed by the numerous battles and fires that have taken their toll throughout the years of Kyoto's history.

fig. 1.4 (opposite) *Map of Japan showing its relationship to the Asiatic mainland.*

fig. 1.5 *Climatic factors in present-day Kyoto: average rainfall and temperature. (Source: Kyoto Municipal Government.)*

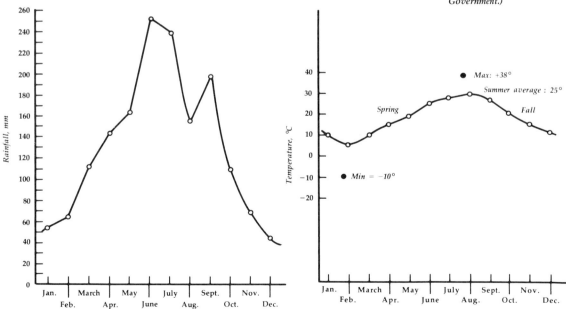

Year	China	Japan				
	Dynasty	Historical Period	Art Period	Event	Cultural Trend	Garden
500		Prehistoric Age	Yamato	Buddhism introduced via Korea in 552		
			—552—			
	—618—	Ancient Age	Asuka		Strong influence of Chinese culture	
	T'ang		—710— Nara	Nara becomes capital in 710		
			—794—	Kyoto becomes capital in 794	Flowering court culture	Shinden style architecture and gardens develop 1052 Byodoin
	—907— Five Dynasties		Heian		Rise of distinctly Japanese art forms	
1000	—959— Northern Sung				Rise of Pure Land and other forms of popular Buddhism	
	—1126—		—1185—			
	Southern Sung	Medieval Age	Kamakura	Military government established at Kamakura in 1185	Strong influence of Zen on culture	1227 Sakuteiki written
	—1208— Yuan (Mongol)			Kyoto again political focus. Ashikaga military government		1339 Saihoji 1397 Kinkakuji
	—1368—		—1392— Muromachi	Onin War, most of Kyoto destroyed in 1467		
				Collapse of central government in 1477		
	Ming			Civil War		1482 Ginkakuji 1488 Ryoanji 1513 Daisen-in
1500			—1568— Momoyama	Hideyoshi assumes control in 1582	Development of the Way of Tea	1598 Sambo-in
			—1615—	Edo (Tokyo) becomes political focus in 1615		
		Premodern Age	Edo	Shogun closes Japan to outside world in 1639	Emergence of popular culture	1624 Shodenji 1639 Entsuji 1641 Shisendo 1643 Kohoan
	—1644—			Perry forces Japan to sign trade treaty in 1854		
1900	Ch'ing (Manchu)	Modern Age	—1867— Meiji		Strong influence of Western culture	
	—1911— Republic					

HISTORICAL DEVELOPMENT

For the purpose of an overview, Japanese history can be broken down into five major ages: the Prehistoric Age preceded the coming of Buddhism and Chinese cultural influence; the Ancient Age saw the initial close imitation of Chinese civilization give way to distinct Japanese forms under a central court nobility; the Medieval Age was marked by competing military groups wrestling for power; in the Premodern Age, a stable feudal state headquarters was established in Tokyo; and the Modern Age began shortly after Commodore Perry forced Japan to begin commerce with the outside world. Figure 1.6 shows that the gardens of this survey span a 300-year history which falls into the Medieval and early Premodern ages. Within these ten gardens, three principal yet overlapping phases of development can be recognized.

The first gardening phase was a modified form of the paradise style garden which had developed earlier, during the Ancient Age. The second phase consisted of the miniature landscapes that were built in the fifteenth and sixteenth centuries around Zen temples. The third phase included the garden settings meant to recreate the wilderness around a hermit's retreat. These three phases of gardening—the paradise model, the Zen stone landscapes, and the tea garden—are dealt with in detail in Chapter 14, but some introductory words are in order here.

The original paradise style gardens surrounded the aristocratic mansions of the Heian period (784–1185). These mansions, known as *shinden*, combined a number of corridor-linked buildings that bordered on a southern pond (Fig. 14.3). A unique and enduring feature of this style was water side pavilions connected to the main compound by covered bridges (Figs. 1.7, 1.8, and 1.9). The image of paradise stems both from the life-style of the courtiers, given over to elegant pastimes amid rich and colorful settings, and from descriptions of the Buddhist Pure Land: a paradise filled with sensuous rewards for the faithful. The gardens of Saihoji (Ch. 2), Kinkakuji (Ch. 3), and Ginkakuji (Ch. 4), and to a lesser extent Sambo-in (Ch. 7), contain elements which are carry-overs of this *shinden* style. Functioning as part villa and part temple, the compound offered its makers (members of the ruling aristocracy) splendid buildings erected amid a garden containing rare and beautiful plants and animals. People enjoyed boating parties on the pond; they were

fig. 1.6 (opposite) *Historical table.*

fig. 1.7 (below) *Detail of Kasuga-gongen-reikenki (Kasuga picture scroll, 1309) showing the waterside pavilion.*

fig. 1.8 (bottom) *The foundation of the Kinkakuji's Golden Pavilion (1397, rebuilt 1955). (Photo by Ryusaku Tokuriki.)*

fig. 1.9 *The Sambo-in tea house of the nineteenth century continues in the tradition of waterside construction.*

serenaded by musicians as they floated around the small islands in ornate boats.

Other elements in the same gardens indicate that garden imagery began to turn away from an otherworldly vision of paradise to one that celebrated a more earthly beauty—hence the name, modified paradise style. Saihoji, which is divided into two parts, quite clearly shows this dual nature. The lower garden with its "golden" pond once contained many fine buildings and flowering trees in the paradise fashion, while the upper garden, resting in an evergreen surrounding and with its dry stone composition symbolizing a waterfall, shows the beginning of a kind of landscape gardening which became equated with the gardens of Zen monasteries.

The gardens of Kinkakuji and Ginkakuji offer other variations on this theme, though both were patterned after Saihoji. The pavilions that remain today in these two gardens are copies of those once found in Saihoji before their destruction in the fifteenth century. The Kinkakuji, with its Golden Pavilion and grand pond, combines paradise elements with a Chinese grandeur that was fashionable at the time. Ginkakuji (Silver Pavilion) with its smaller

scale, diminutive buildings, and miniature stone bridges shows a design attitude closer to the more realistic style found in Zen temple gardens, while still containing many paradise style derivatives. The Shogun who built the Ginkakuji, Ashikaga Yoshimasa, was a patron of Zen and the arts, a devotee of garden making, poetry, and Noh drama; he was also an important figure in the development of the "way of tea." His reign marked the autumnal years of Ashikaga family control, a period of both cultural harvest and political decline. Even as Ginkakuji was being built, the country plunged into civil wars that were to last over a century.

During the wars, the Buddhist monasteries continued to function as repositories of scholarship and culture. The monks studied Chinese learning and, in the Zen temples, practiced a style of landscape painting which had developed in Sung China. These same monks also made simple gardens recreating— with sand, stones, and a few plants—landscape scenes similar to those of the Chinese paintings. Ryoanji (Ch. 5) and Daisen-in (Ch. 6) are two such Zen gardens using a technique called *karesansui* (dry gardening). Literal in the sense that they often portrayed actual landscapes, yet abstract in that they used miniature elements and sand to symbolize water, like the upper garden of Saihoji, they demonstrate the Zen preference for finding beauty in the things of this world.

The third phase in garden making begins after the consolidation of power on a national level in the late sixteenth century. This was accomplished by a succession of military leaders, Oda Nobunaga, Toyotomi Hideyoshi, and Tokugawa Ieyasu, who finally succeeded in overcoming all rival feudal lords. Hideyoshi (1536–1598), a man who had risen through the ranks from the lowest class to become Nobunaga's first lieutenant, assumed control when Nobunaga was assassinated in 1582. This "big hearted son of the soil" began an impressive building program of palaces, castles, and temples, partly as a display of political power and partly as a means of impoverishing his rivals.[3] His garden at Samboin (Ch. 7), built ostensibly for a cherry blossom viewing party, was a similar show of power. The intent of the garden with its grand bridges, powerful waterfalls, and hundreds of stones is quite removed from the tiny landscapes of the Zen monks: He tried to confirm the legitimacy and splendor of his reign by recreating such architectural forms of past glory as the Heian *shinden* mansions.

After Hideyoshi died, the Tokugawa family eventually assumed firm control of a unified Japan. The political focus moved away from Kyoto to distant Edo (modern Tokyo), and the nation sealed itself off from the world to keep out suspected interference. The ensuing 250 years of isolation was an era of relative stability which saw the emergence of a middle class of merchants and artisans. Garden making, which had been the sole province of aristocrats and monks, now fell into the hands of professional craftsmen who catered to the increasing prosperity of the middle class. Though the political and commercial center had moved away from Kyoto, a deep and widespread nostalgia for the old capital remained. Gardens built in Edo or the provinces sought either to recreate famous views in and around Kyoto or to recapitulate famous gardens. The later gardens were sometimes grander in scale and usually incorporated an eclectic mixture of

forms and techniques with little regard for historical or metaphorical integrity.

In the Kyoto gardens of the early Edo years, however, these eclectic mixtures demonstrate a pinnacle or final synthesizing of forms before the onset of an overall degenerating trend toward either stale imitation or flamboyant eccentricity. In the last four gardens of the survey, symptoms of both genius and eccentricity are apparent. The garden of Shodenji (Ch. 8) is a simple sand and clipped-hedge composition *(karikomi)* meant—like Ryoanji—to recall abstract images, yet its materials and composition make it seem more ornamental than profound. Entsuji (Ch. 9) also adopts the rectangular plot of the monastery garden, but here the softer materials of moss and clipped hedges make it seem far less stark and more ornamental than the paintinglike landscapes of earlier temple gardens.

Whereas Shodenji and Entsuji are like final borders of Zen garden prominence, Shisendo (Ch. 10) and Kohoan (Ch. 11) are the introductory phases of the retreat, or tea, garden. Under the Tokugawas, Chinese scholarship and art connoisseurship came out of the temples and entered the secular life. So too did garden making, which adopted scenes typical of a hermit's retreat as the ideal image of nature. This image, coupled with the tea cult, a highly stylized set of related art forms coordinated around a tea drinking ceremony, created a new garden used expressly as a part of the ceremony. The principal feature of this garden—the pathway—served to recreate the sense of journeying to a hermit's hut or tea house. The garden became a setting for the tea house in giving an overall rustic impression. Just the name Kohoan (Hermitage of the Solitary Sampan) gives an indication of how strongly the retreat metaphor affected the design.

Thus, these ten examples trace the complete redefinition of a garden as it went from the rendition of a heavenly paradise to a miniature landscape, and on to a setting for a retreat. The architectural image changed from a gold-covered pavilion to a thatched-roof hut, and the garden went through a similar transition in a way that revealed not only changing attitudes toward nature but also a changing social structure.[4]

By the time Perry reached Japan, in the mid-1800s, garden making had for the most part become an ornamental art. Like Edo period architecture, garden making ceased to evolve and began to filter from the highest classes to other levels of society. Once contact with the outside world was established, a tide of Western teachings, artifacts, and technologies swept through Japan, profoundly altering the physical environment. Changes in life-style were also mirrored in garden designs that added Western elements to an already eclectic repertoire. The resulting confusion was widespread, both in determination of the overall garden design and in selection of the proper materials and symbolic forms. Architects and designers have been trying ever since to fashion an appropriate garden synthesis, one that would express the modern Japanese relationship to nature while still offering the essential satisfaction of the traditional designs.

NOTES

[1]Andrew Boyd, *Chinese Architecture 1500 B.C.–A.D. 1911*, Alec Tiranti, London, 1962.
[2]Teiji Itoh, *Kenchikugakutaikei (Encyclopedia of Architecture)*, vol. 2, Shokokusha, Tokyo, 1969.
[3]Wm. Theodore de Bary (ed.), *Sources of Japanese Tradition*, vol. 1, Columbia, New York, 1958, p. 312.
[4]For the best concise description of Japanese history see G. B. Sansom, *Japan: A Short Cultural History*, Tuttle, Tokyo, 1931, 1976.

part one

The Gardens

chapter two

Saihoji

NAME *Saihoji means the Temple of the Western Fragrance, but its popular nickname is Kokedera (Moss Temple).*

HISTORICAL CONTEXT AND CONTINUITY

Although much changed from its original appearance, the garden of Saihoji is one of the oldest surviving in Japan. Temples have occupied the same site since the eighth century, but the reconstruction of 1339–1341, attributed to the Zen monk Muso Kokushi (Muso the National Teacher, 1275–1351), established the general plan and some of the details seen today. Starting with the remnants of a Pure Land temple, Muso erected many buildings which were named after those mentioned in an important Zen Buddhist text.[1] These multistory buildings differed from the previous one-story buildings of the early *shinden* style, and one of them, the Shariden (Reliquary Hall), served as the model for both the Golden Pavilion of Kinkakuji and the Silver Pavilion of Ginkakuji. Like those of the *shinden* style, the buildings were dispersed among the garden and were connected by covered corridors which bridged the pond (Fig. 2.7). All of the original buildings were destroyed in 1469 during the Onin Wars, and those now found in the compound date from the seventeenth century onward. The garden and pond too have been changed by periodic floods (Plate 1). Today the garden has a rustic, overgrown kind of beauty due in part to the many reconstructions and intermittent periods of neglect. The enormous trees and forest atmosphere seem more in keeping with a Western park than with the closely manicured and restrained feeling of most Japanese gardens. The once-splendid compound, filled with bright plants and magnificent buildings, is now a place of quiet tranquillity on a hillside from which the works of man have almost disappeared.

fig. 2.1 *Late eighteenth-century wood-block print of Saihoji.*

GENERAL DESCRIPTION

Saihoji is a large garden by Japanese standards; it covers over 4.5 acres (18,211 square meters) set against a forested hillside and appears to continue into the woods without boundary. It gives one the overall impression of being in a deep, spacious forest surrounded by a sea of green. The nickname Moss Temple comes from the numerous types of moss covering most of the garden floor. This moss, together with some low rocks, small shrubs, and an occasional tree stump, makes up a lush miniature landscape that carpets the ground. Towering overhead, a ceiling of broad evergreens keeps the garden in perpetual shade. At eye level the garden is relatively free of vegetation, allowing a clear view through many tree trunks which increases the sense of depth. Only a few 6 to 8 foot maples in the lower part of the garden provide the autumnal show of color that contrasts strikingly with the evergreen enclosure. The majority of trees in the garden are not trained to specific shapes, as in later gardens, but are allowed to grow naturally.

fig. 2.2 (below) *Plan of Saihoji site and surroundings.*

fig. 2.3 (right) *Saihoji plan.*

Scale m: 0   2   10

N

The lower part of the garden, centered around a pond with several islands, is separated from the upper dry section by a ceremonial gateway (Fig. 2.11). This division represents the distinction between the older paradise concept of a garden and the later Zen practices (Ch. 14).

The main features of the upper garden are rock compositions designed to suggest water (Figs. 2.13 and 2.14), a technique known as *karesansui* (gardening without water). Taking stones from the surrounding mountains, the makers built a large cascading stonework that suggests the tumble and fall of a forceful waterfall.[2] This is a full-size feature built into the landscape and it is easy to imagine water running through it, though it never did. The composition continues down the hillside to suggest two calm pools; alongside one sits a large flat stone for Zen meditation. Further "downstream" sits another rock composition, this one in the form of a turtle, recalling the Chinese legend of the mystic islands where immortal beings dwelt on islands supported on the backs of huge turtles (Fig. 2.12). The two parts of the garden are also differentiated by the lack of maples in the upper garden. Their bright fall color would contradict the sense of restraint that eliminates the bright and showy. The waterless rocks rest year long in the deep green surroundings.

REMARKS

Saihoji incorporated garden forms and techniques from previous ages and also introduced many innovations. The dry waterfall used in the upper garden was the beginning of a technique and a kind of abstraction that became widely used in Zen gardens. In later gardens, however, the rock composition would be reduced in size from a full-scale landscape feature to that of a model landscape. The pathways offered guests an opportunity to stroll in the garden rather than being confined to boats or corridors as in the past. Such paths became the most important feature of tea gardens two hundred years later. Particular elements of the Saihoji garden—such as its spring, streams, and buildings—were directly copied in other gardens. The genius of Saihoji has continually supplied inspiration for generations of garden makers.

NOTES

[1]Chapter 18 of *Hekiganroku*, translated by Katsuki Sekida in *Two Zen Classics: Mumonkan and Hekiganroku*, Weatherhill, Tokyo, 1977, pp. 194–196.

[2]This usually accepted interpretation was disputed (in a March 1977 conversation with the authors) by Kinsaku Nakane, who believes that the construction is merely part of a staircase.

Saihokawa River

Garden wall

Islands

fig. 2.4 *Saihoji section.*
Note: *The vertical scale is magnified 50 percent.*

Dry
waterfall

Upper garden

Ceremonial
gateway

Golden Pond

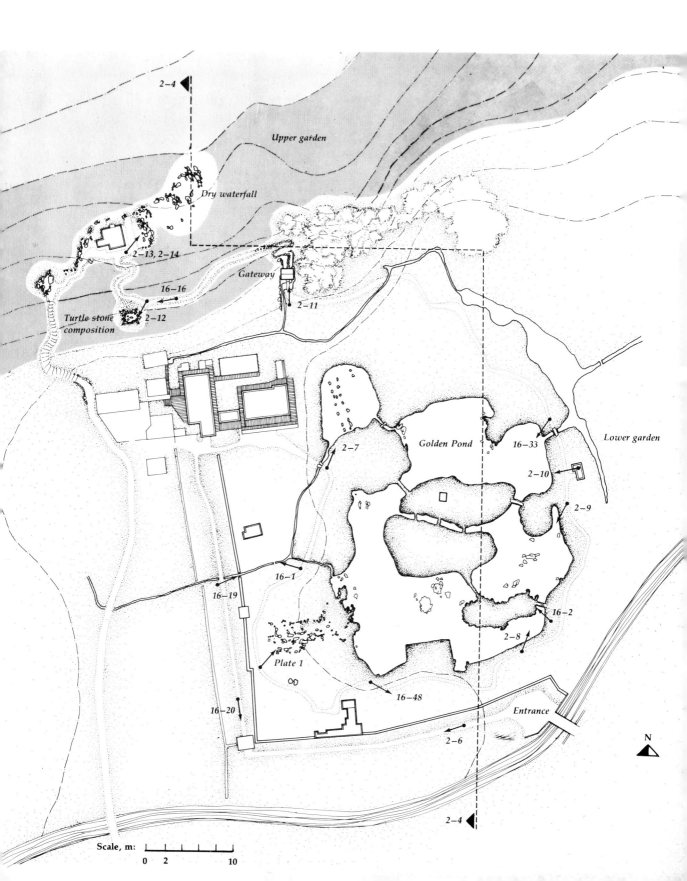

2–4

Upper garden

Dry waterfall

2–13, 2–14

16–16

Gateway

2–11

Turtle stone
composition

2–12

Golden Pond

16–33

Lower garden

2–7

2–10

2–9

16–1

16–19

16–2

2–8

Plate 1

16–48

16–20

Entrance

2–6

2–4

N

Scale, m:

0   2   10

fig. 2.5 (opposite page) *Saihoji conceptual plan. (On this and all other schematic plans, the numbers indicate photo illustrations.)*

fig. 2.6 (above) *Saihoji entrance pathway.*

fig. 2.7 (below) *The foundation stones for the covered bridge that once connected the buildings of Saihoji. These stones have also been interpreted as the former moorings for the pleasure boats that were used for outings in the garden.*

Saihoji / 21

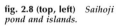

fig. 2.8 (top, left) *Saihoji pond and islands.*

fig. 2.9 (top, right) *Another view of the same pond.*

fig. 2.10 (circle) *View from inside the tea house.*

fig. 2.11 (bottom) *The gateway that separates the lower and upper gardens.*

fig. 2.12 (top) *Stone composition resembling a turtle. The head is rising on the right, while a foreleg is closest to the viewer.*

fig. 2.13 (center) *The dry waterfall.*

fig. 2.14 (bottom) *Detail of the dry waterfall showing the support work for the major stones.*

chapter three

Kinkakuji

NAME *The Rokuonji (Deer Park Temple) contains one of Japan's most famous buildings. It is a three-story pavilion covered with gold leaf, which gives the temple its nickname, Kinkakuji (Temple of the Golden Pavilion). Its real name, the Deer Park Temple, refers to the deer park near Benaras, India, where the Buddha gave his first sermon on enlightment.*

HISTORICAL CONTEXT AND CONTINUITY

Medieval Japan was characterized by both political turmoil, as rival military clans competed for supremacy, and intense artistic creativity. The Ashikaga family first succeeded in gaining power in 1338 and held marginal control for 150 years. Having reestablished Kyoto as their capital, the Ashikaga reinstituted official trade with China, which had all but been abandoned for centuries. During their reign, the second great wave of Chinese culture swept through Japan. Whereas the first wave, which had come in with Buddhism in the early centuries of the Ancient Age, had its roots in T'ang culture, this second wave was an echo of the great Sung Dynasty (Fig. 1.6). Under the Ashikaga, who were patrons of both the Zen sect of Buddhism and the arts, Japanese culture attained new levels of sophistication. Ashikaga Yoshimitsu (1358–1408) was the third of the Ashikaga family shoguns but the first to show an interest in art and culture. In his enthusiasm for the Chinese style, he occasionally wore Chinese style clothing and had himself transported by Chinese palanquin. When he decided to relinquish his title officially, in a manner recalling that of the Heian emperors (Ch. 14), he built a large *shinden*-like compound in 1394 on the site of a ruined thirteenth-century villa.

fig. 3.1 *Late eighteenth-century wood-block print of Kinkakuji.*

Like the "fishing" pavilions of the *shinden* style, the Golden Pavilion (Fig. 3.7 and Plate 3) used to sit surrounded by water, linked to the other buildings by a corridor attached to its second story. The silt of the centuries has filled in the pond between the waterfall and the building, so that it now stands on the bank of the pond. The pond, like the waters of the Heian gardens, was used originally for boating parties (Fig. 3.9).

The eclectic and ornate architecture of the Kinkakuji reflects a period when new influences were being digested and assimilated with past forms of glory. In actual form the Golden Pavilion is based on a building from Saihoji (Shariden), but the top story of the Golden Pavilion with its black lacquered floor definitely followed the style of the times. It is generally assumed that the shogun, a man of taste and connoisseurship, acted as his own designer. When the Chinese ambassador came for an audience, the retired shogun is said to have mentioned the stone composition representing the center of the universe, called the "Nine Mountains and Eight Seas," in the pond (Fig. 3.12). In so doing, he compared the presence of the two great men in the garden to that of the sun and the moon revolving around the cosmic center.

Like Saihoji, most of the compound was destroyed during the Onin Wars of 1467–1477, with only the Golden Pavilion and the pond surviving intact. In 1950 it too was destroyed, and a faithful replica was erected in 1955.[1] The present main temple buildings and the tea house and its garden were added in the early 1600s by the Emperor Gomizuno (Ch. 9).

GENERAL DESCRIPTION

The Kinkakuji is a large compound (230,000 square meters) which contains a wide entryway, an assortment of buildings, and two ponds (Fig. 3.5). The upper pond apparently dates from the first villa on this site; the lower one, though somewhat altered in form and reduced in size, is all that remains of the shogun's original compound. This lower pond—with its standard southern orientation, islands of dwarf pine trees, and impressive stoneworks—is the most interesting part of the garden. The pines, along with the large numbers of stones in the foreground, greatly increase the sense of the pond's depth (Fig. 1.8).

Behind the pavilions lie a moss-and-tree forest and two water features, a spring and a waterfall (Fig. 3.10 and Plate 2), that were based on the Saihoji model. They are fed by the overgrown older pond, which lies on a terrace above. At a yet higher point are a large tea house and a modest tea garden (Figs. 3.6 and 3.11). A garden within a garden, this small space is highly structured for the necessities of the tea ceremony and is quite different in scale and intention from the original compound.

REMARKS

Kinkakuji demonstrates the continuing influence of the Saihoji model (the buildings, water features, and so forth), modified to suit the then-ruling tastes for things Chinese and opulent. The scale of the garden is grand by Japanese standards, and surviving gardens built in subsequent times, until the Edo period, were substantially smaller. As the garden stands today, it is almost a museum of gardening techniques and structures thrown together without any clear meaning.

NOTES

[1]For a dramatization of the arson which destroyed the Kinkakuji, see Yukio Mishima, *The Temple of the Golden Pavilion*, translated by Ivan Morris, Tuttle, Tokyo, 1959.

fig. 3.2 *Plan of Kinkakuji site and surroundings.*

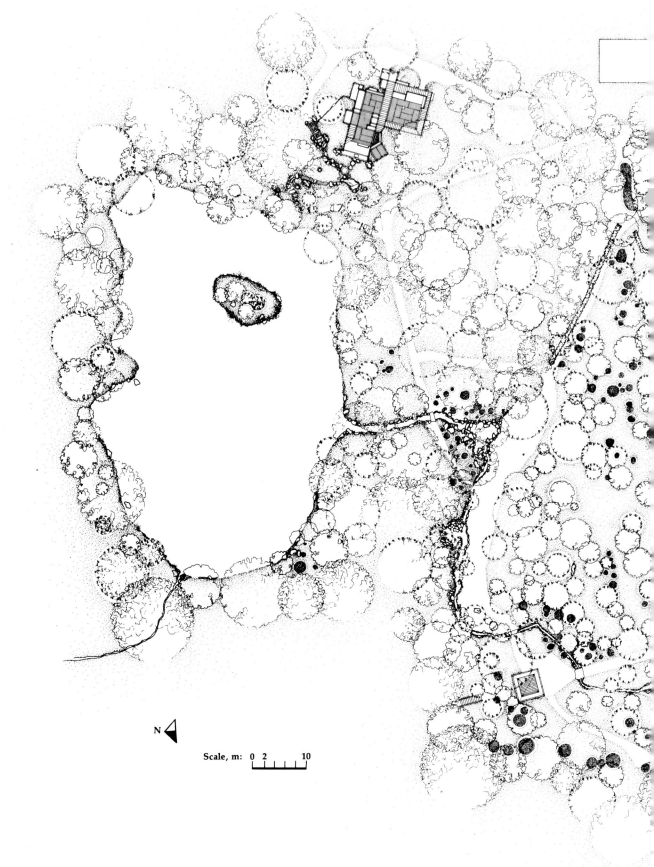

N

Scale, m: 0 2   10

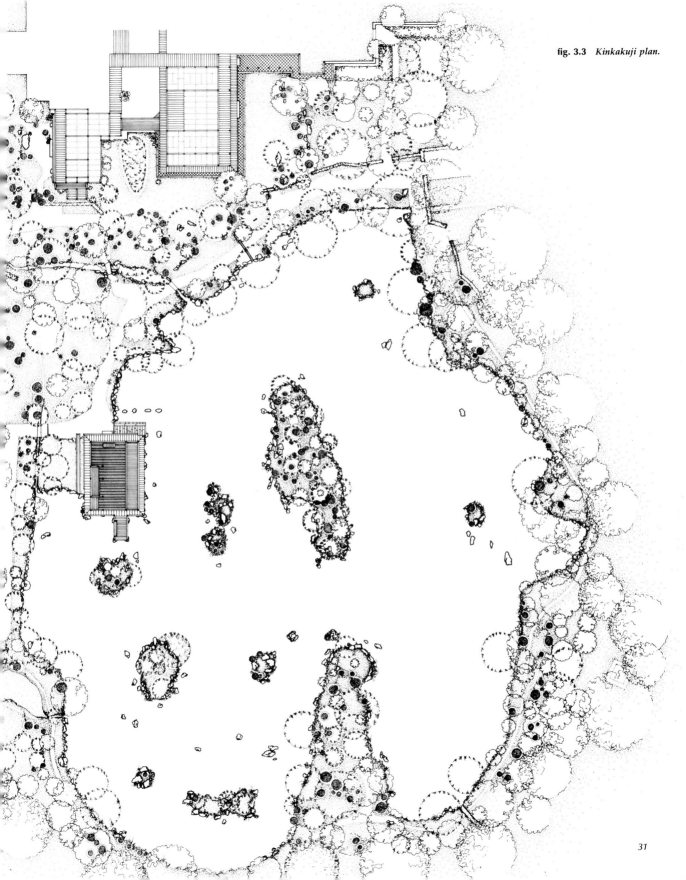

fig. 3.3 *Kinkakuji plan.*

31

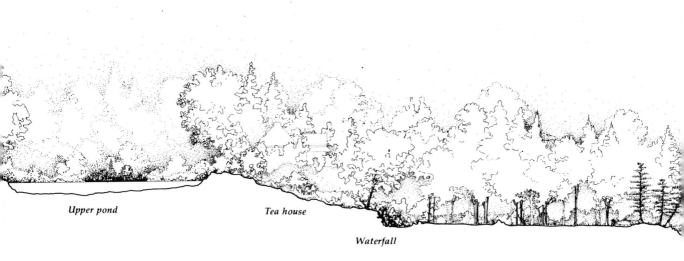

Upper pond

Tea house

Waterfall

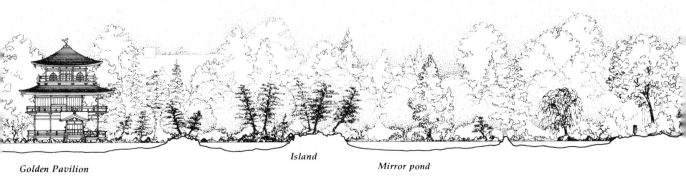

Golden Pavilion

Island

Mirror pond

fig. **3.4** *Kinkakuji section.*

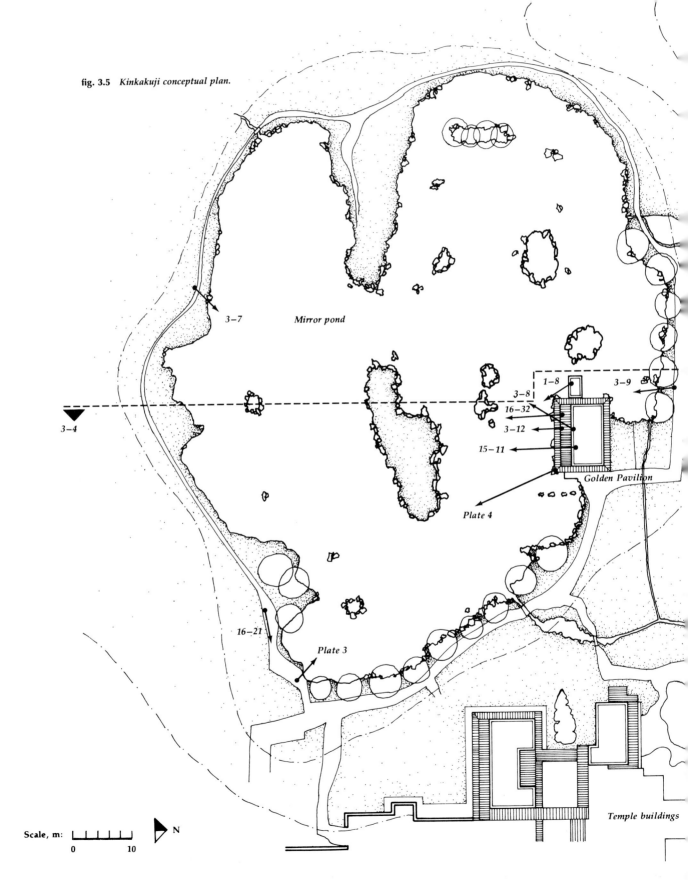

fig. 3.5 *Kinkakuji conceptual plan.*

3-7

Mirror pond

3-4

1-8   3-9

3-8
16-32
3-12
15-11

Golden Pavilion

Plate 4

16-21

Plate 3

Temple buildings

Scale, m:

0   10

N

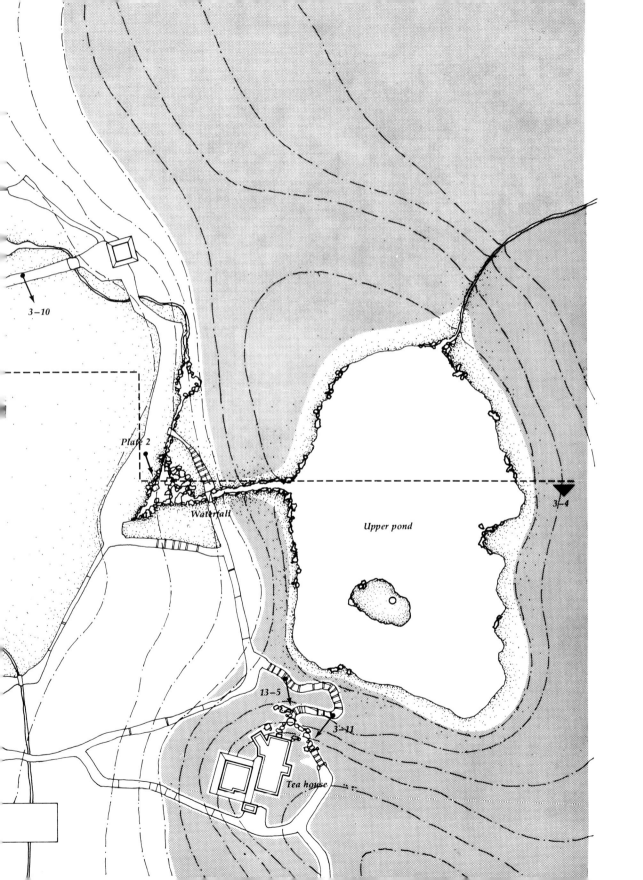

3–10

Plate 2

Waterfall

Upper pond

13–5

3–11

3–4

Tea house

fig. 3.6 (right) *Section of Kinkakuji tea house (early seventeenth century).*

fig. 3.7 (below) *The Golden Pavilion. (Photo by Ryusaku Tokuriki.)*

fig. 3.8 (left, top) *View from the third floor of the pavilion overlooking the pond and a distant mountain. Legend has it that when the shogun felt oppressed by the summer heat, he had this mountain draped with white silk to remind him of snow. (Photo by Ryusaku Tokuriki.)*

fig. 3.9 (left, center) *Boats are still stored under the side extension, which is reminiscent of the* **shinden** *style fishing pavilion.*

fig. 3.10 (left, bottom) *Behind the Kinkaku (Golden Pavilion) is a forest area that looks much like Saihoji.*

fig. 3.11 (right, upper) *The tea house in the upper garden.*

fig. 3.12 (right, lower) *The stone composition surrounded by water is the "nine mountains and eight seas" symbol for the center of the universe.*

chapter four

Ginkakuji

NAME *Within the compound of the Jishoji (Light of Mercy Temple) there is a small building known as Ginkaku (Silver Pavilion). The pavilion's name comes from the legend that its builder intended to plate the inside of the second floor with silver. The temple has thus become popularly known as Ginkakuji (Temple of the Silver Pavilion).*

The garden and buildings were constructed on the grounds of an earlier temple during the years 1482–1492. Its builder was Ashikaga Yoshimasa (1435–1490), grandson of the builder of Kinkakuji, who continued the family tradition of supporting the arts. Although the design of the garden has been traditionally attributed to his tea master, Shuko (1422–1502), it is now generally accepted that the garden was designed by Yoshimasa himself, together with Zenami, a member of the lowest social class, who actually managed the labor.

The garden of Ginkakuji, like that of its predecessor, Kinkakuji, was based on the Saihoji model and is similarly divided into two parts (Fig. 4.5): the pond, buildings, and maple trees in the lower garden (Plate 6); the stone composition and spring above (Fig. 4.11). When Ginkakuji was built, appreciation of the Saihoji garden had become something of a cult, and Yoshimasa visited it many times before he built his own garden. Construction of his villa temple was interrupted by the devastating series of Onin Wars that left most of Kyoto, including Saihoji and Kinkakuji, in ruins. Rival feudal lords were contesting each other for power, and the Ashikaga shogunate was unable to enforce order. An uneasy peace was established during the 1480s, and Ginkakuji was completed. Its comparatively small scale is in some way indicative of the decline of the family power. Yet an increasing sense of restraint, partially the result of Zen standards of discipline seen in all the arts of the period, probably had some impact in shaping the overall diminutive form of the compound.

fig. 4.1 *Late eighteenth-century wood-block print of Ginkakuji.*

During the years following Yoshimasa's death, all of the buildings burned—except the Ginkaku pavilion and the Togudo (East Seeking Pavilion), both replicas of buildings found in Saihoji—and some of the trees and garden rocks were carried off to make other gardens, most notably that of Nijo Castle. When the Ginkakuji was rebuilt in 1629, new buildings were erected and the white sand bed and cone replaced some of the burned buildings. Woodcuts of the garden show these two features growing successively larger as the years went by until they reached today's proportions. The gardens behind the new buildings also date from this later period. The upper garden remained in ruins until it was rebuilt in 1931.

GENERAL DESCRIPTION

The east–west axis of the Silver Pavilion forms a principal organizing factor in the garden. Inside the second story sits a Pure Land Buddhist statue that looks out through Zen style windows (cusped arch) over the garden and the enclosing hillside (Plate 8). The ravine along this axis is called the moon viewing crack because the harvest moon is said to rise between its two slopes (Fig. 4.16). A waterfall called the "moon washing" fall is located along the same line, 30 meters in front of the pavilion (Fig. 4.9). This is also the distance between the waterfall and pavilion at Kinkakuji. In both instances, the waterfall is designed to provide an echo chamber so that the sound is easily heard inside the pavilion.

The view from the pavilion is truly overwhelming (Figs. 4.14 and 4.17). Its beauty comes in part from the hillside, a tapestry of various trees under cultivation, and from the careful organization of the garden which blends with the surroundings. All the pine trees in the garden are trained at an incline to lead the eye up the hillside. A round "moon" stone rests in the pond "above" the reflected hillside, thus appearing to float in the reflected heavens (Fig. 4.15). A band of maples at the base of the hillside provides the fall colors (Plate 6).

The pond itself is quite small and surrounded by numerous stones which appear as miniature mountains (Fig. 4.10). The uncut stone bridges have a model-like quality but are still suitable for human use (Figs. 16.3, 16.4, and 16.5). Both the white sand bed and cone seem like abstract sculptures when compared to the overall realistic landscape-in-miniature of the original garden (Fig. 4.8). It has been suggested that the sand bed's original purpose was to reflect moonlight onto the pavilion itself.

The other original building, the East Seeking Pavilion, was rebuilt in the late 1960s (Fig. 4.13). The pond in front of this building is almost a separate garden within itself and is oriented on an approximate north–south axis. This building contains the prototypical tea room, embodying a format which had a lasting effect on Japanese architecture. In it are found the standard four-and-one-half tatami-mat room and the *tokonoma* (ritual alcove) that became a standard part of the Japanese house.[1]

REMARKS

The Ginkakuji garden marks the culmination of early Japanese gardening elements and the beginning of later ones. The lake is too small for boating and thus becomes merely ornamental; strolling is a more suitable way to see the garden. Here, in its pathways, small scale, and emphasis on detail, are rudiments of the tea garden which developed during the hundred years after the tea ceremony was first initiated at Ginkakuji.

NOTES

[1] A. L. Sadler, *Cha-No-Yu: The Japanese Tea Ceremony*, Tuttle, Tokyo, 1962, pp. 94–97.

fig. 4.2 *Plan of Ginkakuji site and surroundings.*

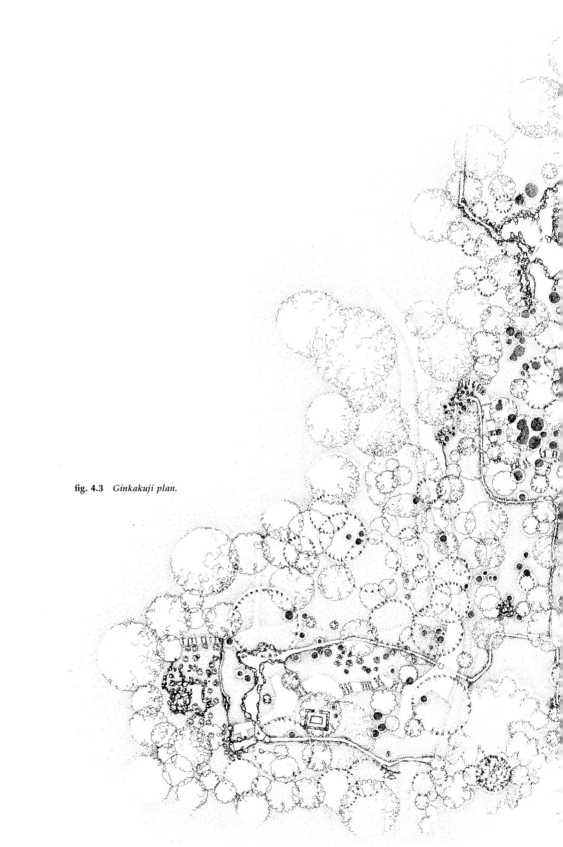

fig. 4.3 *Ginkakuji plan.*

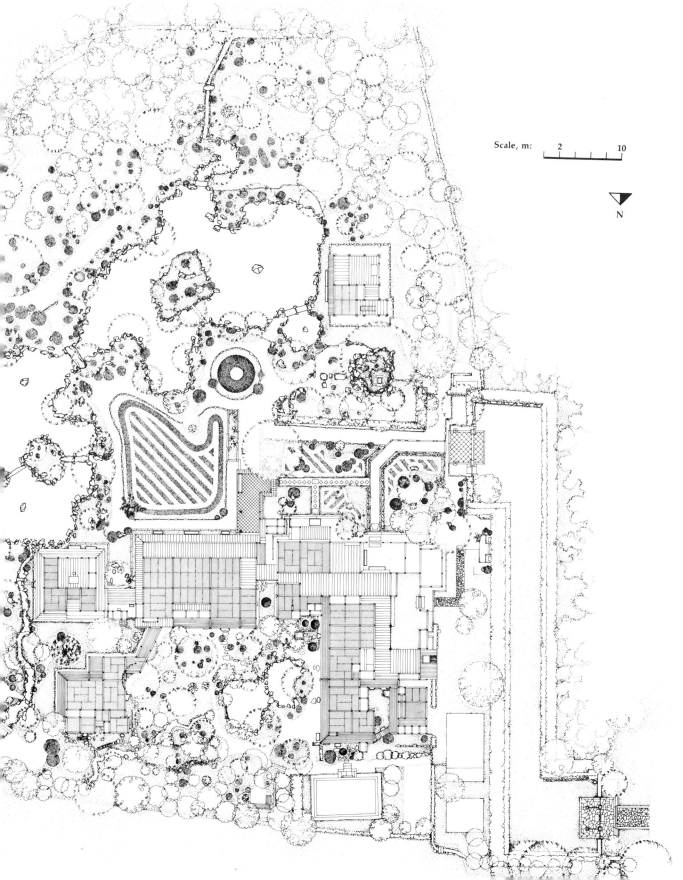

Scale, m: 2   10

N

Upper garden

Pond and islands

fig. **4.4** *Ginkakuji section.*

Sand bed and cone   *Silver Pavilion*   *Entrance pathway*

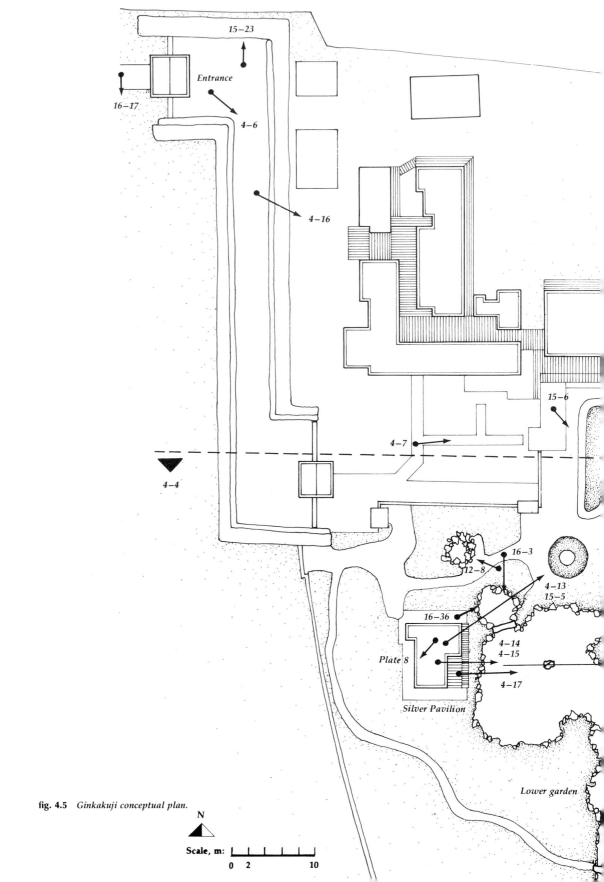

15–23

16–17

Entrance

4–6

4–16

4–4

4–7

15–6

16–3

12–8

4–13
15–5

16–36

4–14
4–15

Plate 8

4–17

Silver Pavilion

Lower garden

fig. 4.5 *Ginkakuji conceptual plan.*

N

Scale, m:

0   2   10

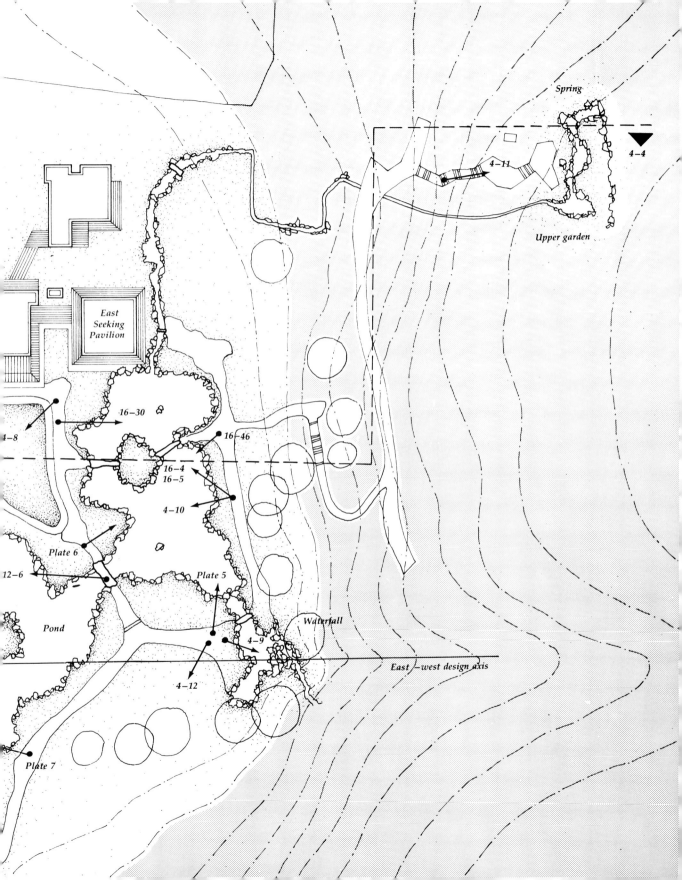

Spring

4–4

4–11

Upper garden

East
Seeking
Pavilion

16–30

16–46

4–8

16–4
16–5

4–10

Plate 6

12–6

Plate 5

Pond

Waterfall

4–9

4–12

East —west design axis

Plate 7

fig. 4.6 (top, left) *The entrance pathway to Ginkakuji.*

fig. 4.7 (top, right) *Entry garden and gate to inner garden.*

fig. 4.8 (center) *The modest two-story Silver Pavilion beyond the white sand bed and cone.*

fig. 4.9 (bottom) *The "moon washing" waterfall.*

fig. 4.10 (above) *General view of the northern part of the garden shows the pond, stonework, and meticulously trimmed black pines that are the principal features of Ginkakuji.*

fig. 4.11 (left) *The hillside stonework of the upper garden.*

fig. 4.12 (top, left) *The moss-covered area of the lower garden again is like that of Saihoji.*

fig. 4.13 (left) *The Togudo (East Seeking Pavilion) seen from the Silver Pavilion.*

fig. 4.14 (top, right) *The enclosing eastern mountain seen from the Silver Pavilion.*

fig. 4.15 (top, left) *The moon stone. If the photograph is viewed upside down, the moon appears to be rising above the hillside.*

fig. 4.16 (top, right) *Moon rise above the eastern mountain.*

fig. 4.17 (left) *View from the ground floor of the Silver Pavilion. The ice- and snow-covered pond here looks strikingly like the later white sand gardens.*

plate 1 *Former part of the Saihoji pond is now covered by moss.*

2

4

3

5

6

7

plate 7 *The Silver Pavilion (Ginkakuji) in winter.*

plate 8 *The Amida Kannon sculpture in the Silver Pavilion is the western terminus of the garden's east—west design axis.*

8

plate 9 *Just as the stones can
be likened to mountains,
the moss at Ryoanji
can become a miniature forest.*

plate 10 *A scene in
the Daisen-in miniature
landscape.*

9

10

11

plate 11 *The pond and earthen bridge are the principal components of the Sambo-in main garden.*

plate 12 *The small tea garden in the rear part of Sambo-in.*

plate 13 *The hand-washing basin in the tea garden of Sambo-in, symbolizing the moon, is located within the pond.*

12

13

plate 14 *Overall view of Shodenji. Notice how the plants both inside and outside the garden progress in height from left to right.*

plate 15 *The Entsuji garden incorporates Mt. Hiei into the composition.*

14

15

16

17

plate 16   *As one moves downward through the clipped azaleas, the inner garden of Shisendo is completely obscured from view. Notice also the eclectic use of roof materials and the unique second-story lookout.*

plate 17   *The rounded, clipped hedges in the post-1940s lower garden of Shisendo produce a highly ornamental effect.*

plate 18   *The ever-open entryway to the bosen room (right side of picture) seen from the pathway of Kohoan.*

plate 19   *This dwarf pine increases the sense of depth in Kohoan.*

18

19

chapter five

Ryoanji

竜安寺

NAME *Ryoanji (Peaceful Dragon Temple).
The dragon is a symbol with many meanings
in East Asia, most of which are related
to power and energy. The dragon can,
for example, symbolize the Emperor or it can
represent the energy in the earth (Ch. 13).*

HISTORICAL CONTEXT AND CONTINUITY

The earliest temple recorded on this site dates from 983. Like Saihoji and Kinkakuji, it was destroyed during the Onin Wars. It is believed that the garden was laid out during the rebuilding of 1488. Although it was created at approximately the same time as Ginkakuji, it represents the new kind of gardening fostered by the Zen monks. It is believed that many similar gardens were built at that time, but only Ryoanji has survived intact. Its origin most likely lies in a mixture of sources—the small tray gardens of China and Japan (Fig. 5.6), the pure pebble ground coverings of sanctified Shinto precincts, and the style of landscape painting preferred by Zen monks. Its original form and intention are still subject to debate, with some experts claiming that it once contained trees and plants and has recently been simplified.

Nor is it possible to attribute the garden to any one designer. Popular tradition has it that Soami (1480?–1525), an artist also associated with Daisen-in, made the garden. Conflicting temple records name other makers, while the back of one stone is inscribed with the names of Kotaro and Hikojiro, two laborers who probably did the actual construction and perhaps even helped in the design.

The records are more conclusive about the temple buildings. The main building burned in 1789, and a substantially larger structure was moved here from another site. The east side of the garden had to be shortened to make room for a new gate that was added at the same time. In 1977–1978, both the roof of this relocated building and the garden wall were repaired. The clay-tiled roof of the wall was replaced with one of cedar shingles, and the texture of the wall was significantly changed.

fig. 5.1 *Late eighteenth-century wood-block print of Ryoanji.*

GENERAL DESCRIPTION

These fifteen stones, arranged into five groups upon a rectangular bed of white sand (336.6 square meters), have provoked more commentary and speculation than perhaps any other single Japanese garden. They are often used to illustrate the profound mysteries found in Zen Buddhism and as an example of the unique Japanese design spirit. There is no shortage of theories to explain the garden's mysterious appeal, ranging from historian Loraine Kuck's description of the "sermon in the stone" and its occult balance to the more prosaic Japanese folk explanations of a tiger crossing the river with her cubs, mountaintops above the clouds, or islands in the sea.[1] Indeed, these many possible meanings form a large part of its appeal.

All the stones, except one, seem to be flowing from left to right. The relationship among groupings is a fine example of asymmetric balance (Ch. 15).

REMARKS

Ryoanji demonstrates a level of abstraction and sophistication far beyond that of its predecessors. The once mandatory feature of an East Asian garden, the pond, has been eliminated completely, and *karesansui* (dry gardening) has developed into a technique suitable for an entire garden instead of just a single feature. The garden's overall simplicity, the elimination of trees and plants, and high level of abstraction reflect the impact of Zen and its inspired search for the essential in art (Ch. 14).

NOTES

[1]Loraine Kuck, *The World of the Japanese Garden*, Walker/Weatherhill, Tokyo, 1968, pp. 163–171.

fig. 5.2 *Plan of Ryoanji site and surroundings.*

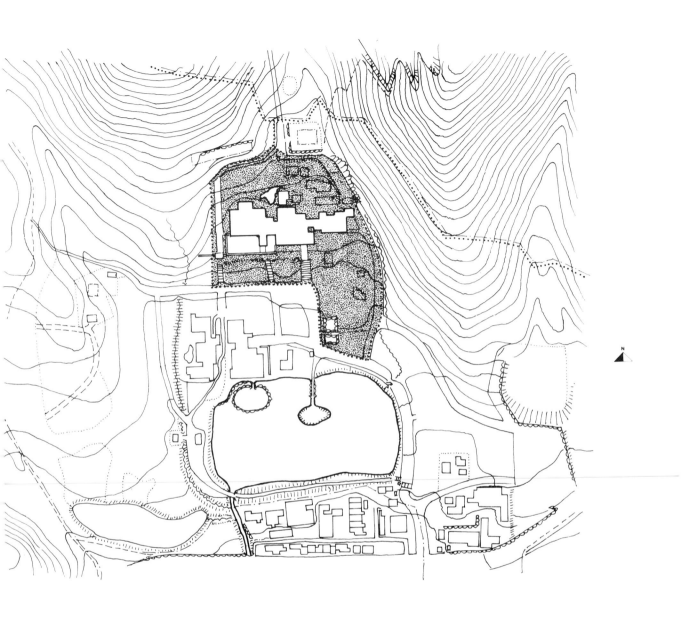

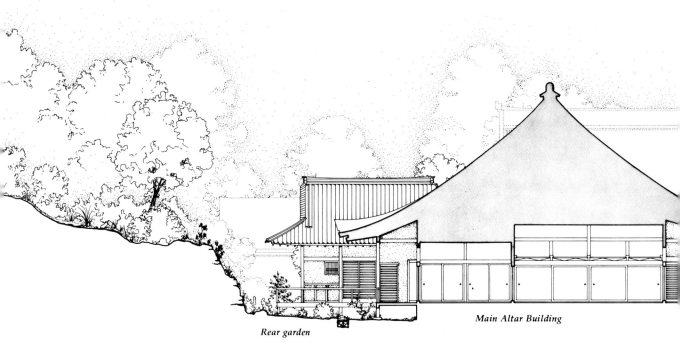

Rear garden

Main Altar Building

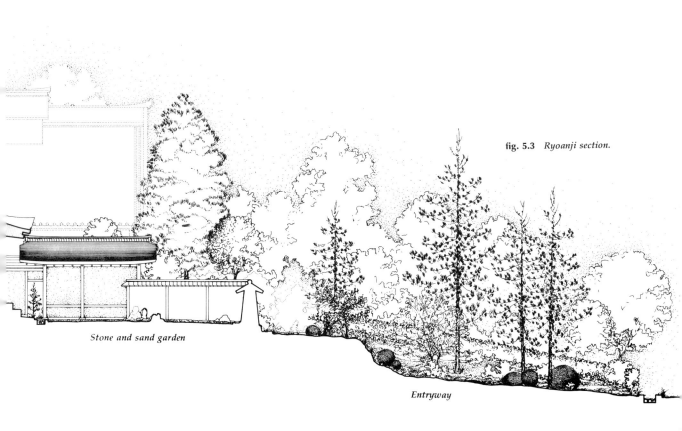

Stone and sand garden

Entryway

fig. 5.3 *Ryoanji section.*

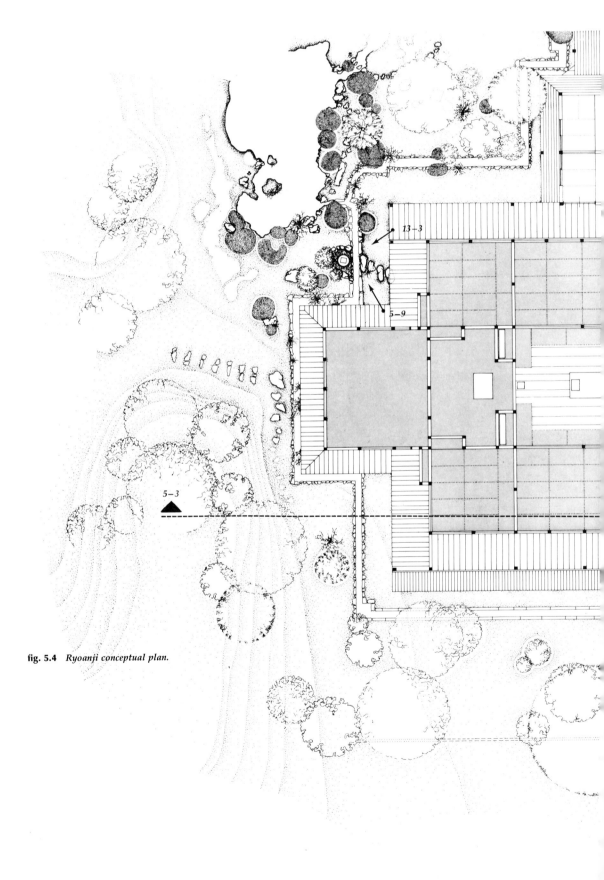

13 — 3

5 — 9

5 — 3

fig. 5.4 *Ryoanji conceptual plan.*

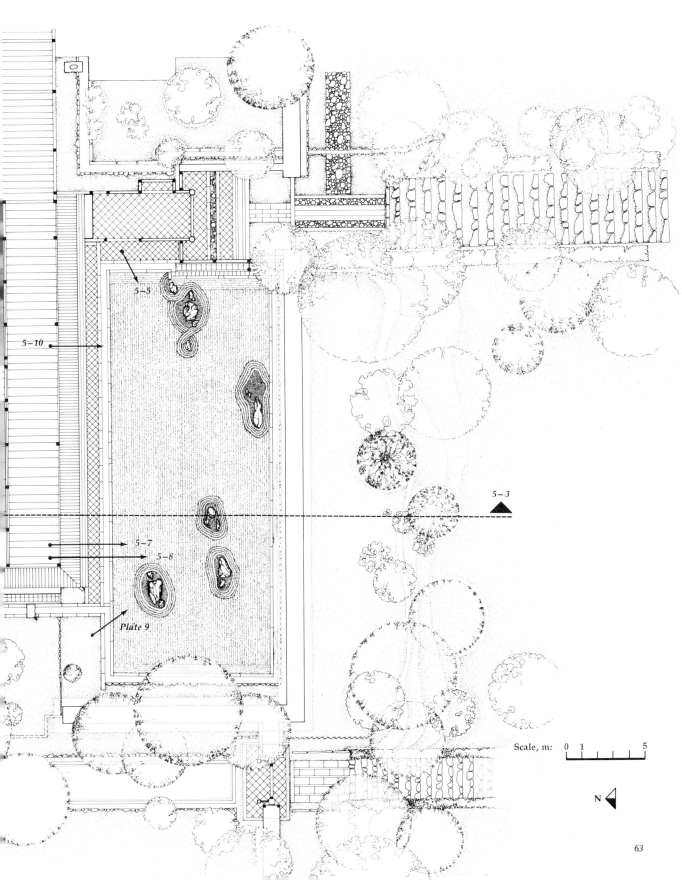

5-5

5-10

5-3

5-7

5-8

Plate 9

Scale, m: 0 1 5

N

63

fig. 5.5 (top) *Overall view of the Ryoanji stone garden.*

fig. 5.6 (right) *Detail from Kasuga-gongen-reikenki (Kasuga picture scroll, 1309) showing a small tray garden. Notice also the bamboo aviary in the background.*

fig. 5.7 (left) *The stone groupings on the garden's west side.*

fig. 5.8 (directly below) *Detail of Fig. 5.7.*

fig. 5.9 (below, left) *The rear garden.*

fig. 5.10 (bottom) *A gravel trough that acts as a rain gutter forms the edge of the sand garden.*

chapter six

Daisen-in

大仙院

NAME *Daisen-in is a subtemple of the great metropolitan Zen temple of Daitokuji. Its name can be translated as the Great Hermit Temple, or the Great Immortal Temple.*

HISTORICAL CONTEXT AND CONTINUITY

Daisen-in was built during the hundred years of civil war that followed the Ashikaga shogunate's loss of power in the early fifteenth century. It was a period of economic hardship and insecurity during which the Zen compounds offered relative security. The temple was originally built to house the retired abbot of Daitokuji, Kogaku Sotan (1465–1548). The main building was built in 1510, the *shoin* in 1514, and the garden shortly thereafter. One report indicates that the garden could have been moved from an estate of a samurai warrior named Mibuchi, but the maker of the garden remains unknown. It is usually attributed to a painter, gardener, and Noh artist named Soami (1480?–1525) whose landscape paintings decorate the sliding paper doors of the temple (Fig. 6.12). It is now generally assumed that Kogaku Sotan and Soami together planned the garden and that the actual work was done by some laborers known to have worked at setting stones in Ginkakuji and Ryoanji.

This garden seems to have survived reasonably intact without major changes since its construction. Following World War II, the main building was restored, the southern garden was built, and both moss covering the sand and a hedge covering the wall were removed. Additionally, a corridor alleged to be original was rebuilt (Fig. 6.5), but its authenticity and the overall impact remain objects of contention.

fig. 6.1 *Late eighteenth-century wood-block print of Daisen-in.*

GENERAL DESCRIPTION

Daisen-in, like Ryoanji, is a dry landscape garden that takes its form from ink monochrome landscape paintings. Unlike Ryoanji, which portrays a single scene, Daisen-in resembles the typical long scroll rolled from right to left to reveal a sequential painting illustrating a journey through the countryside. Daisen-in's rectangular format causes the viewer to scan horizontally across the scene, with the white wall in the background mimicking the unpainted silk of a landscape scroll (Fig. 15.13).

The scene's main focus is in the northeast corner, where several large stones represent tall mountains (Fig. 6.6). Terraces of white sand form a simulated waterfall, the apparent source of a twin-branched sand stream (Fig. 6.7). One branch of the "stream" runs along the north edge of the building, passing stones resembling cliffs until it reaches a functional drainage area of gray pebbles (Fig. 6.8). Here is an early form of the hand-washing stone arrangement that became a standard feature of tea gardens a hundred years later. The other branch of the stream "flows" southward along the building's eastern edge through a simulated mountain valley that includes bridges and pathways, cliffs and islands, and even a stone shaped like a cargo junk. This stream terminates at the southern garden, which is simply a large rectangular bed of white sand now said to represent a great sea (Fig. 6.9). The raked bed is barren except for a single tree and two white sand cones that recall the Shinto salt cones of purity.

Along with the obvious scenic references, Japanese monks—writing after the garden was made—attributed certain cosmologic implications to Daisen-in. In their view, the size and relative position of the stones correspond with the domain and relative importance of certain deities of the Buddhist pantheon. Thus, they saw the garden as a kind of three-dimensional mandala, or literal diagram, of the religious universe. How much this interpretation is a projection of meaning, rather than an original intention, remains to be established.

The garden contains many symbolic landscape features that come out of a variety of gardening and religious traditions. Its crane and turtle islands (Fig. 6.5), for instance, are symbols of longevity of the type particularly favored in temple gardens supported by the warrior class. The stone mountain in the northeast, the favored direction for large mountains (Ch. 13), is an allusion to the central mountain Shumisen of Buddhism. The river is compared by the present monks to the river of life, its condition reflecting the human condition as we age and flow toward the great sea of nothingness.

Despite its literalness, the Daisen-in garden displays considerable artistry in selection and use of stones and achieves a sense of great depth for such a small space. The garden employs many techniques of landscape painting and miniaturization.

REMARKS

Both Daisen-in and Ryoanji are dry Zen gardens *(karesansui)*, but they differ considerably in overall effect. Daisen-in is a much more obvious attempt to recreate a shrunken landscape. It has the kind of lighthearted playfulness that characterizes later gardens, and also reflects an overall trend in gardening toward smaller scale and finer details.

fig. 6.2 *Plan of Daisen-in site and surroundings.*

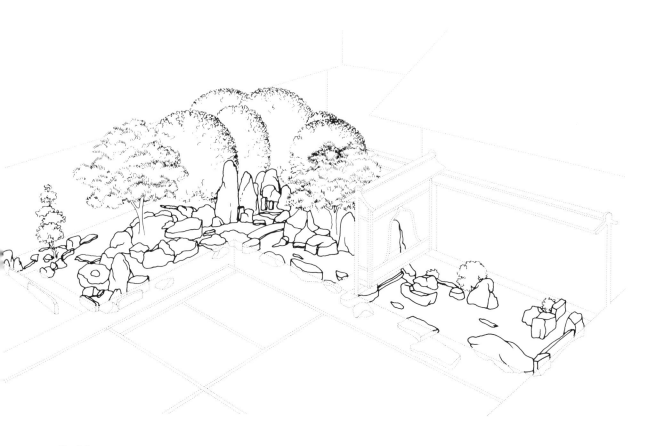

fig. 6.3 *Perspective drawing of Daisen-in's main garden.*

Sand and stone garden

Sand cone and bed

Entrance

fig. 6.4 *Daisen-in section.*

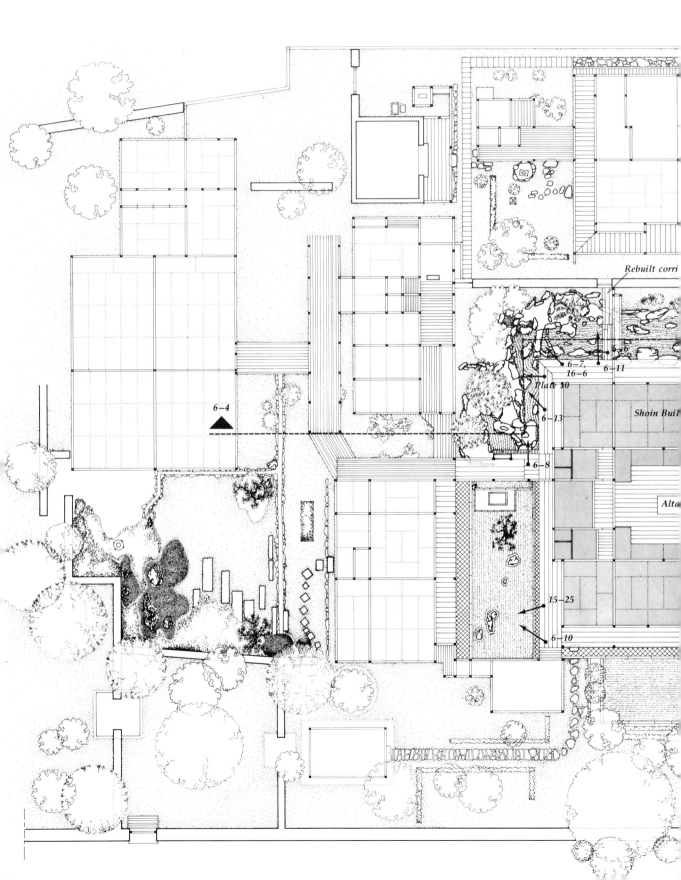

Rebuilt corri

6–7,
16–6
6–11

Plate 10

6–13

Shoin Buil

6–8

Alta

15–25

6–10

6–4

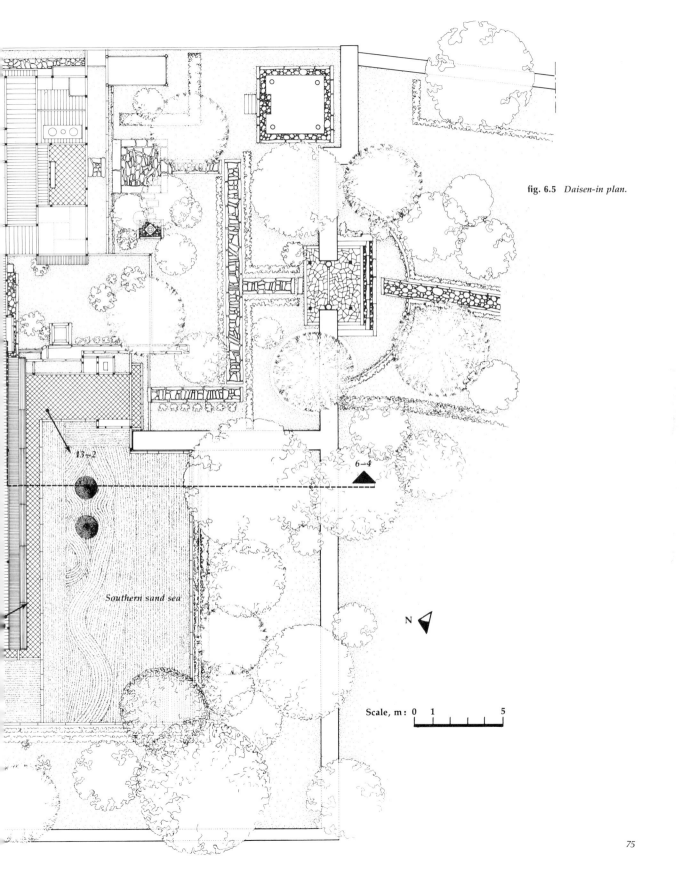

fig. 6.5 *Daisen-in plan.*

13–2

6–4

Southern sand sea

N

Scale, m: 0   1   5

THIS PAGE:

fig. 6.6 (top) *The garden's main focus.*

fig. 6.7 (center) *The terraces of white sand represent the cascades of a waterfall.*

fig. 6.8 (bottom) *An early form of hand-washing basin. Water remains in the hollow of the stone at the left, while the gray pebbles on the right side form the drainage area.*

OPPOSITE PAGE:

fig. 6.9 (top, left) *The great sand sea of the sourthern garden.*

fig. 6.10 (below, left) *The rear garden.*

fig. 6.11 (top, right) *The structure of this one-meter stone gives a realistic impression of a mountain.*

fig. 6.12 (below, right) *The* **fusuma** *(interior sliding paper doors) are painted with landscape scenes by Soami.*

fig. 6.13 (bottom) *A turtle-shaped island seen with its rear leg closest to the viewer and its head rising in the right-hand corner.*

chapter seven

Sambo-in

NAME *Sambo-in is a subtemple of Daigoji.
Its name refers to the three Buddhist
treasures: the Buddha, the law,
and the priesthood.*

HISTORICAL CONTEXT AND CONTINUITY

During his rule of Japan in 1582–1598, Toyotomi Hideyoshi undertook an impressive building campaign. He wrote, "I mean to do glorious deeds . . . and to return in triumph and leave a great name behind me."[1] Along with Sambo-in, he built Osaka Castle and his grand castle at Momoyama, for which the historical period is named. Once he established control over a unified Japan, his dreams of power encompassed all of Asia and he launched two invasions into Korea. Near the end of his life he decided to go and view the famous cherry blossoms at Daigoji; that too was done with characteristic extravagance. He had buildings specially built and ordered the Sambo-in garden constructed in thirty-six days. To accomplish this task in so short a period required hundreds of workers. At one time as many as 2000 men were working on the project. Feudal retainers were compelled to donate stones and trees for the garden. Such items were highly prized: Garden stones were considered jewels and each one carried a pedigree showing its lineage of ownership. One such stone—the Fujita stone (Fig. 7.12)—was moved "wrapped in silk, decorated with flowers and brought to the garden with the music of flute and drums and the chanting of laborers."[2]

Hideyoshi worked with the chief abbot of the temple, Gien Jugo, on the original design. Once the great outing was over, Gien's journal records how he and a succession of gardeners labored for twenty-eight years to bring the garden to perfection. The main waterfall, for example, was rebuilt three times during those years (Fig. 7.10). The dean of Japanese garden historians, Mirei Shigemori, wrote that the garden failed to make a satisfactory harmonic impression just because it was overworked by so many different artisans. Gien, he argued, was a client who could never decide what he wanted and therefore wound up with a collection of many different styles.[3]

Hideyoshi's cherry blossom viewing pavilion originally sat on the nearby mountainside but was subsequently moved inside the temple (Fig. 7.6). Numerous other buildings and gardens have been added to the compound in the succeeding years, with the Imperial gateway relocated from east to south. The main south garden, however, has survived intact from Gien's time and is the best representative garden from the Momoyama age. It remains something of a testament to Hideyoshi's love of glorious display.

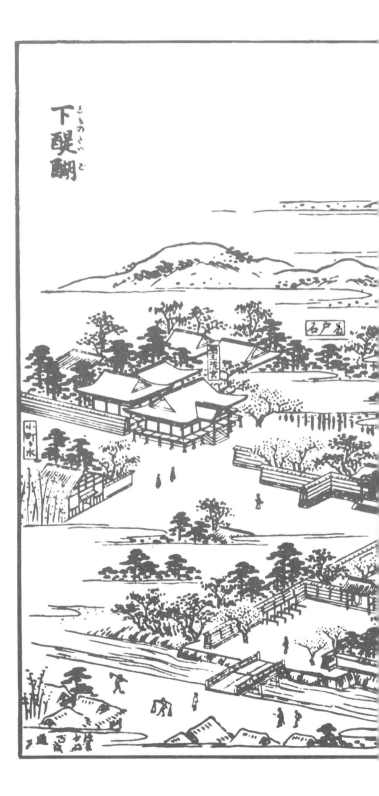

fig. 7.1 *Late eighteenth-century wood-block print of Sambo-in.*

GENERAL DESCRIPTION

The most striking thing about the main garden is its enormous number of stones: Whereas Ryoanji has 15, Sambo-in has over 800 in an area of 5280 square meters. Stones are mostly used here as symbols of wealth and power rather than as model landscape features. Here the bridges of earth, stone, and finished wood reveal a more aggressive attitude about the place of human works in the landscape.

The overall format of the garden, with its southern pond and long pavilion (omote shinden), recalls once again the early shinden style. The "Very Pure View" building actually bridges the pond in a shinden manner (Fig. 7.11). The buildings are arranged in a series of progressively higher terraces (Fig. 7.5). Running between the pond and the lower building is a sand "stream" that acts as a pathway and contains stones with textures resembling varying patterns of flowing water (Fig. 7.13). It is interesting to see that the karesansui technique, which was originally intended to act as a symbolic substitute for water, is here used next to the real thing. Obviously, dry gardening features had become a required gardening ornament. The crane and turtle islands found in the pond are also standard garden forms.

The garden wall is obscured from sight by trees whose height is magnified because they are planted atop artificial hills running parallel to the wall (Figs. 15.1 and 15.2). A large number of stones cover a hillside toward the rear of the garden, giving the impression of a natural rock outcropping belonging to the foothills in the distance (Fig. 15.3).

Other parts of the compound added in later years reveal quite a different spirit. Two such examples are the famous moss and sand composition, resembling sake cups and a gourd (Fig. 16.50) and the little tea garden behind the blossom viewing pavilion (Plate 12). The cups and gourds have a simplicity and literalism not at all in keeping with the style of the original; they may even be the result of European influence. The tea garden's small scale and standard form is completely different from the main garden's overwhelming exuberance and originality, the dainty tea garden bridge having little in common with the massive bridges in the front garden.

REMARKS

The main garden of Sambo-in combined many previous garden forms into one bright and bold display. Obviously the overall spirit is quite different from that found in Zen gardens: Sambo-in belongs to an older, esoteric sect of Buddhism (Shingon-shu), one given to more elaborate art forms. The garden's size and spirit reflect the power and wealth of its patron, who used it as a means of personal and political expression. It provides an interesting contrast to the restrained Zen and tea cult aesthetic that dominates the majority of Japanese gardens built around the turn of the seventeenth century.

NOTES

[1]G. B. Sansom, *Japan: A Short Cultural History*, Tuttle, Tokyo, 1931, p. 413.
[2]Gien Jungo Nikki *(Gien's Daily Record)* as cited in Loraine Kuck, *The World of the Japanese Garden*, Walker/Weatherhill, Tokyo, 1968, p. 182.
[3]Mirei Shigemori, *Nihon Teien Shi Zukan (Illustrated History of Japanese Gardens)*, Momoyama Era Part 2, Yukosha, Tokyo, 1937, pp. 35–41.

fig. 7.2 *Plan of Sambo-in site and surroundings.*

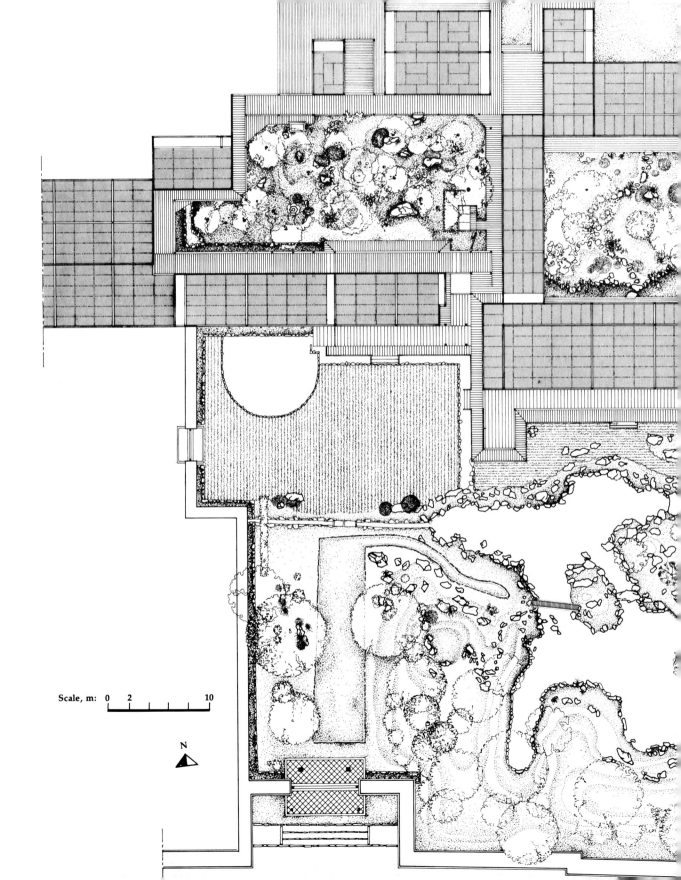

Scale, m: 0 2 10

N

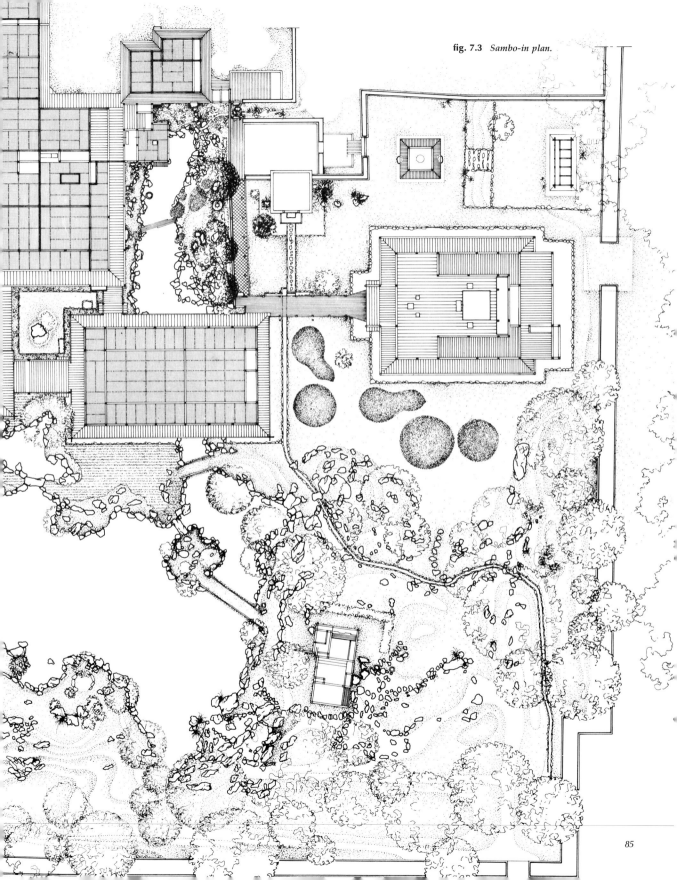

fig. 7.3 *Sambo-in plan.*

Shrine

Altar Building

Reception rooms

Omote shinden

Garden wall

Islands

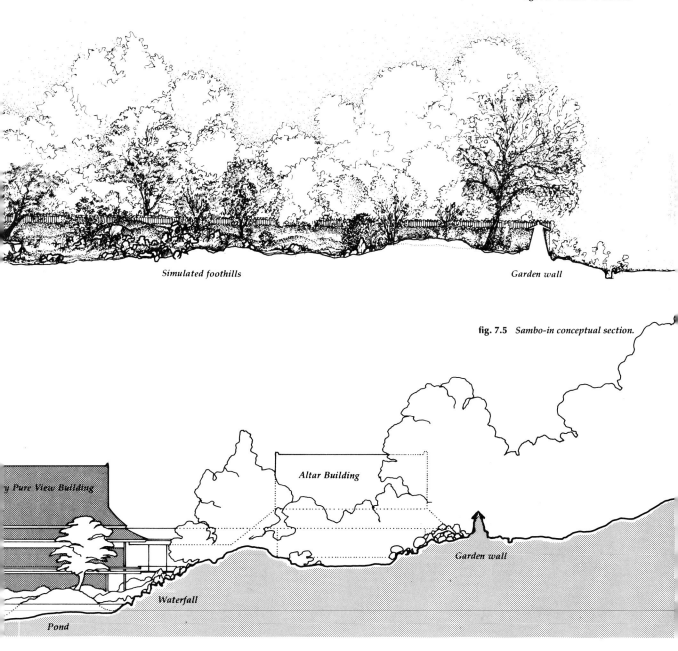

fig. 7.4 *Sambo-in section.*

Simulated foothills

Garden wall

fig. 7.5 *Sambo-in conceptual section.*

Pure View Building

Altar Building

Garden wall

Waterfall

Pond

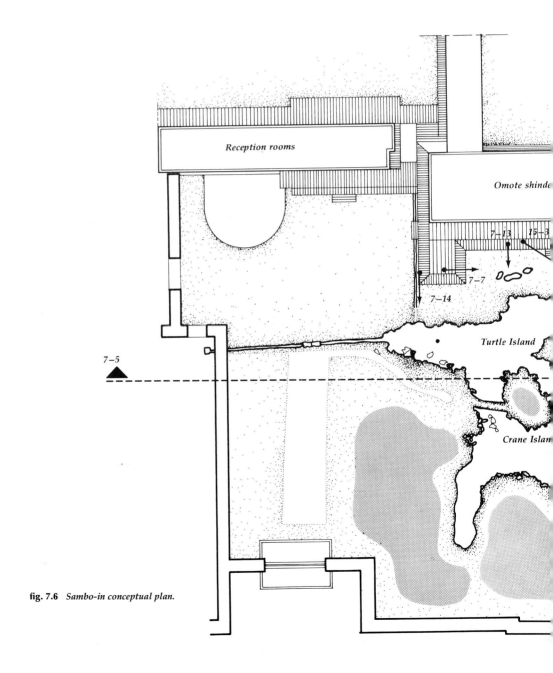

Reception rooms

Omote shinde[n]

7–13   15–3

7–7

7–14

7–5

Turtle Island

Crane Islan[d]

fig. 7.6 *Sambo-in conceptual plan.*

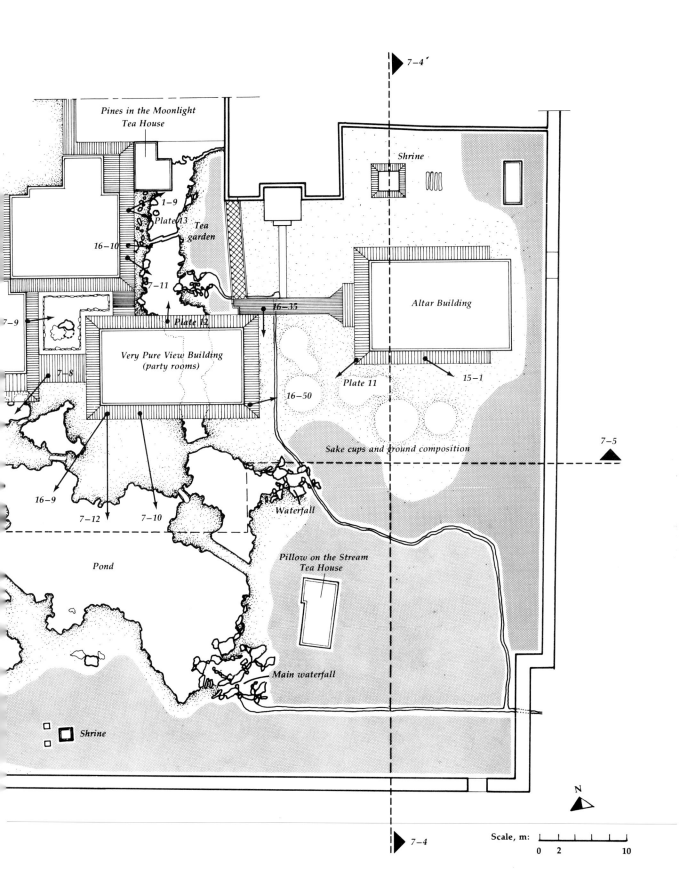

Pines in the Moonlight
Tea House

Shrine

1–9

Plate 13 *Tea
garden*

16–10

7–11

Altar Building

7–9

Plate 12

16–35

Very Pure View Building
(party rooms)

Plate 11

15–1

7–8

16–50

16–9

Sake cups and ground composition

7–5

7–12   *7–10*

Waterfall

Pond

Pillow on the Stream
Tea House

Main waterfall

Shrine

7–4'

N

7–4

Scale, m:

0   2   10

THIS PAGE:

fig. 7.7 (top)   *Overall view of Sambo-in main garden in winter.*

fig. 7.8 (center)   *Looking through the veranda that connects the buildings with the main garden.*

fig. 7.9 (bottom, left)   *Simple* tsuboniwa *(courtyard garden) of bamboo and stone.*

fig. 7.10 (bottom, right)   *The main waterfall has three tiers and a much more powerful spirit and sound than those found in earlier gardens.*

OPPOSITE PAGE:

fig. 7.11 (top, left)   *The "Very Pure Blossom View" building bridges the pond like buildings of the* shinden *style.*

fig. 7.12 (top, right)   *The precious Fujita stone is the large rectangular one. Legend has it that the stone is stained by the blood of a fisherman who had explained the stone's secret to a passing feudal lord. It seems that it once stood above the surface of the Fujito strait at low tide, thereby providing a strategic ford. When the lord discovered this he killed the fisherman lest he divulge the secret to anyone else. Later this same stone came to be used in many gardens before finding its final home at Sambo-in.*

fig. 7.13 (center)   *The fluid texture of this stone adds another layer of symbolism to the dry garden. It is one of the "three stones of the Kamo river" composition meant to express different characteristics of the flowing river.*

fig. 7.14 (bottom)   *The first sago palms imported from southern regions to be used as garden ornaments came to Kyoto around the time Sambo-in was built.*

chapter eight

Shodenji

NAME *The name Shodenji means the Temple of the Correct Tradition.*

HISTORICAL CONTEXT AND CONTINUITY

Both Toyotomi Hideyoshi (Sambo-in) and
Ashikaga Yoshimitsu (Kinkakuji) had
worshipped at the old temple of Shodenji. In
1634 the building was moved from the central
city to the northern outskirts of Kyoto. The
garden is said to have been built during the
following year and its maker remains unknown.
Apparently suffering from the loss of powerful
patronage, the temple garden fell into a state of
semi-ruin in later years. During the Meiji
period it was somewhat rehabilitated and rocks
were added to the composition. These rocks
were removed and the garden restored to
something approximating its original condition
in 1936.

Fig. 8.1 *Late eighteenth-century wood-block print of Shodenji.*

DESCRIPTION

It is a simple dry garden laid out on a rectangular bed of white gravel some 200 square meters in area. Upon the bed, clipped azaleas and camellias are arranged in three groups of three, five, and seven plants (Fig. 8–3). This 3:5:7 formula became popular in later gardens as a kind of "golden ratio" for many aspects of garden design.

Because of its overall format and simplicity, this garden has been called a plant version of Ryoanji. This is interesting because it takes the level of gardening to another degree of symbolism. *Karesansui* (dry gardening) sought to represent landscape and water with only sand and rocks, but this garden tries to represent stones in turn with clipped hedges. Such hedges, known as *karikomi*, became increasingly popular during the Edo period. The reasons for this substitution were no doubt partly economic, for the cost of good gardening stones was prohibitive.

The other interesting feature of Shodenji is the way the scenery beyond its walls is incorporated into the composition. Just beyond the tile-roofed white wall, the vegetation rises in height from left to right just as the clipped hedges rise inside the garden. Beyond these nearby trees lies distant Mt. Hiei, whose fine profile is incorporated into the garden design using a technique the gardeners call *shakkei*, or borrowed scenery (Ch. 15 and Plate 14). The manner of borrowed scenery used in Shodenji is relatively simple, especially when compared to the more sophisticated technique used in Entsuji. The top of the wall acts as a simple trim line between the garden and the borrowed scenery.

REMARKS

During the early Edo period, there was a good deal of variation and experimentation in gardening forms of which Shodenji is a highly stylized and individualistic example. It remains a unique period piece, standing apart from the mainstream of garden development.

fig. 8.2 *Plan of Shodenji site and surroundings.*

Clipped shrubs

fig. 8.3 *Shodenji section.*

Hillside

Altar

Shodenji Temple

Sand

99

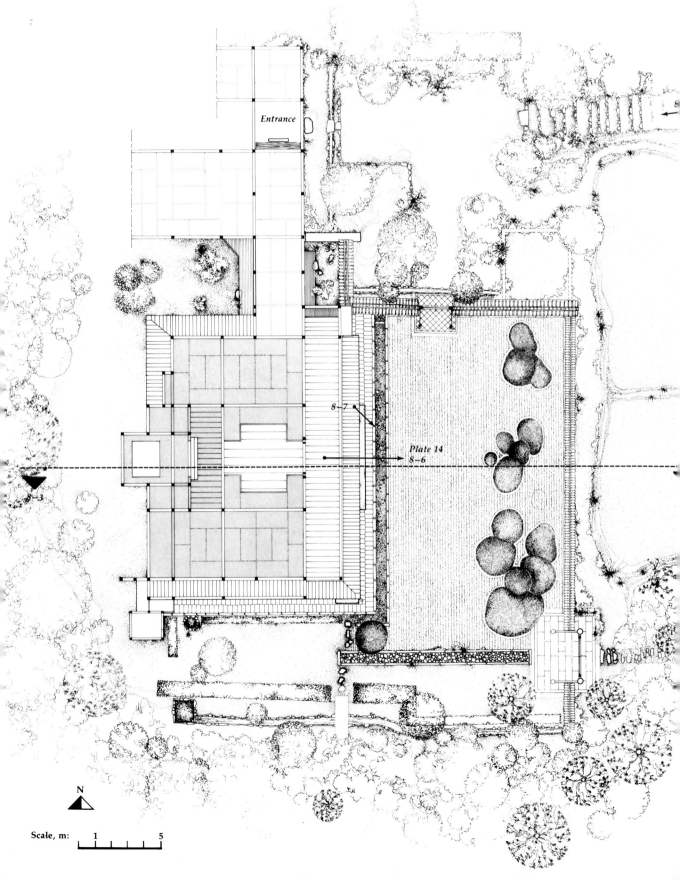

Entrance

8-7

Plate 14
8-6

N

Scale, m: 1   5

fig. 8.4 (opposite page) *Shodenji plan.*

fig. 8.5 (top) *The entrance to Shodenji.*

fig. 8.6 (center) *Detail of the center of the garden.*

fig. 8.7 (bottom) *Side view of the garden.*

chapter nine

Entsuji

NAME *The full name of this temple is Daihizan Entsuji, an abbreviation for one of the names of Kannon Bosatsu, patron goddess of mercy.*

HISTORICAL CONTEXT AND CONTINUITY

In 1615 the political forces moved to Edo
(Tokyo), with the start of the Tokugawa regime,
but the Imperial family remained in Kyoto.
When the Emperor Gomizuno (1596–1680)
abdicated, he first lived in a villa, the location
of present-day Entsuji. When he later moved
on, to the newly constructed Shugakuin villa,
the older site was converted into a Buddhist
nunnery. The garden and main building, which
purportedly came from the Imperial Palace,
have apparently changed little since that time.
Although it now functions as a monastery, the
compound still retains its Imperial affiliations.

幡枝 圓通耲 潮音堂

fig. 9.1 *Late eighteenth-century wood-block print of Entsuji.*

GENERAL DESCRIPTION

Entsuji is a small garden noted primarily for two things: the rock and moss composition within its grounds and the borrowed-scenery view of Mt. Hiei incorporated into the garden composition.

The stone composition is made up of forty-five low stones and two natural rock outcroppings. Closely hugging some of the stones and mimicking their shapes are a few low clipped hedges. The rest of the ground is covered with a rolling carpet of moss. Although the arrangement of the stones seems a little chaotic at first, there is an overall structure. The stones are arranged in three curving rows that diminish in height and number from left to right, the placement meant to recall a flowing river. The major stones—radiating in lines from the center of the viewing room—help to achieve a sense of depth by seeming to create layers (Fig. 9.2).

The low hedge along the rear of the garden serves three main purposes: It is a backdrop for the stone composition; it serves to separate the garden from the numerous trees just beyond the hedge; and it acts as the lower part of the frame that includes Mt. Hiei as borrowed scenery, making it part of the garden composition. Some tall cypress and pine trees stand close to the hedge. The lower edge of their foliage forms the upper part of a frame enclosing the view of the mountain. The tree trunks form the sides of the frame and create a middle ground that draws the mountain into the composition. The mountain on the right of the picture serves as a counterbalance to the numerous stones on the left side of the garden (Fig. 9.2).

REMARKS

Although in keeping with the restrained mood of Zen aesthetics, Entsuji shows considerable softening in design. The moss ground cover (instead of gravel), more rounded stones, and the living hedge substituted for a wall make the garden of Ryoanji seem severe in comparison. Where Ryoanji uses only stones—and Shodenji uses only clipped hedges—Entsuji uses a mixture of both, showing the blending of styles that took place in the early Edo years.

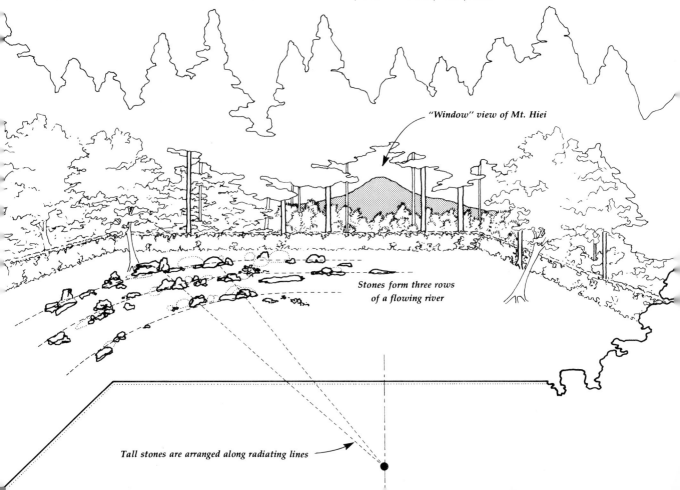

"Window" view of Mt. Hiei

Stones form three rows
of a flowing river

Tall stones are arranged along radiating lines

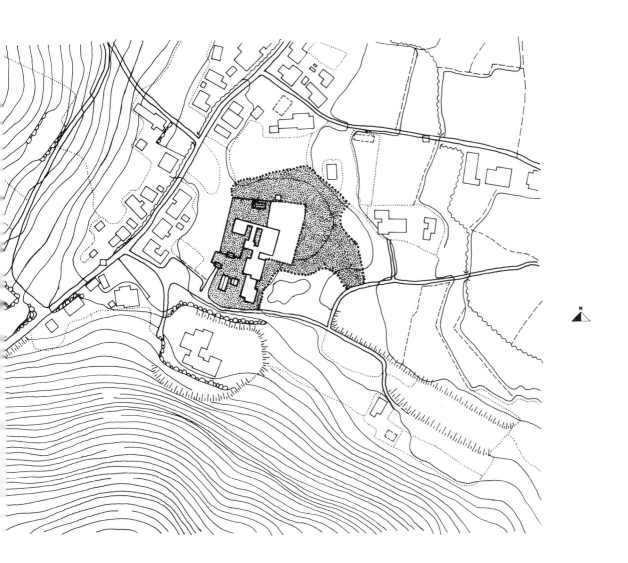

fig. 9.2 (left) *Entsuji conceptual perspective.*

fig. 9.3 (above) *Plan of Entsuji site and surroundings.*

Cypress and crytomeria

Garden

Bamboo grove

fig. 9.4 *Entsuji section.*

Entsuji

Courtyard garden

Altar Building

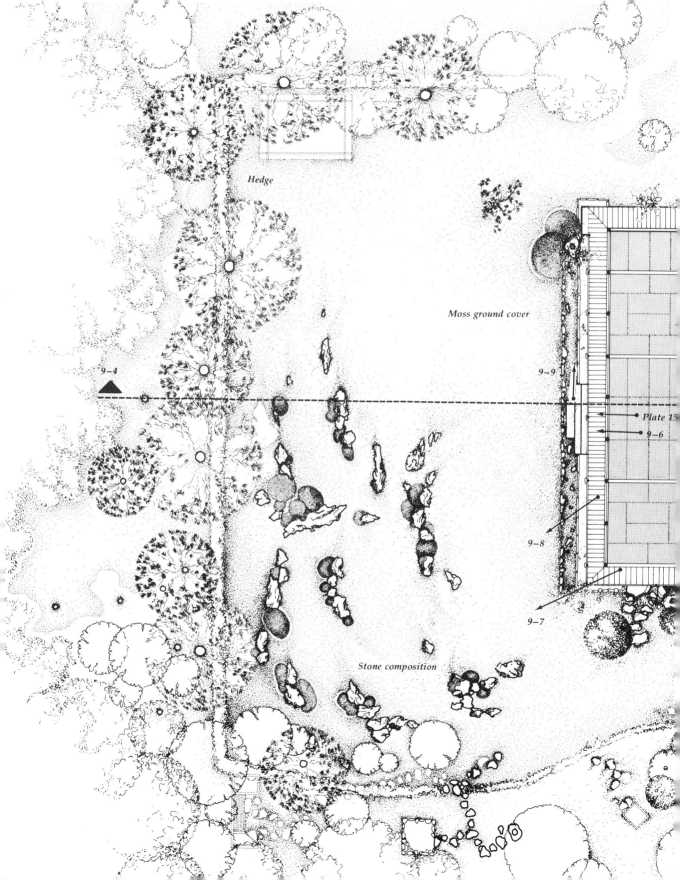

Hedge

Moss ground cover

9-4

9-9

Plate 15

9-6

9-8

9-7

Stone composition

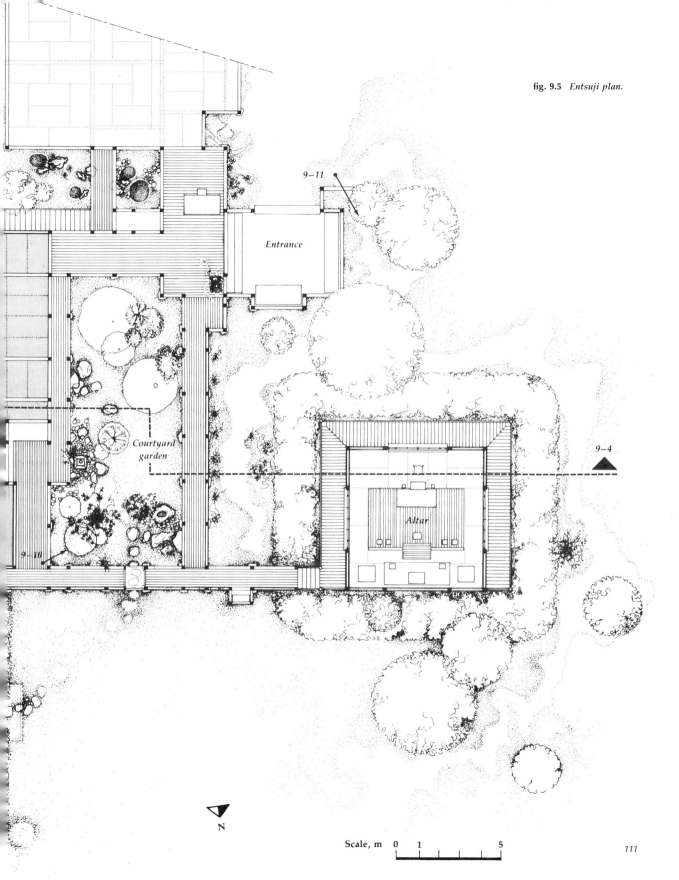

fig. 9.5 *Entsuji plan.*

9–11

Entrance

9–4

Courtyard
garden

Altar

9–10

N

Scale, m   0   1   5

fig. 9.6 (top) *View from inside Entsuji.*

fig. 9.7 (center) *The stonework is concentrated in the northeast corner.*

fig. 9.8 (bottom) *Detail showing the close integration between the clipped hedges and stones.*

fig. 9.9 (top, right) *Wooden rain doors are stored in the box projecting from the wall and can be slid into place along the track on the outside edge of the veranda. Sliding paper doors are used along the inside track of the veranda to form rooms and a corridor.*

fig. 9.10 (top, left) *The recently constructed courtyard garden.*

fig. 9.11 (bottom) *The Buddhist altar building.*

chapter ten

Shisendo

NAME *The name Shisendo can be read as either
Hall of the Hermit Poets or Hall of the Immortals of Poetry.*

HISTORICAL CONTEXT AND CONTINUITY

Legend has it that during the battle of Osaka
Castle, which in 1615 finally established
Tokugawa's position as supreme ruler of Japan,
a samurai warrior named Ishikawa Jozan
(1583–1672) disobeyed his orders to refrain
from battle and charged into the enemy.
Despite Jozan's heroic performance, his initial
disobedience prevented the awarding of any
honors. He resigned disillusioned, eventually to
become a scholar of Chinese classics. He built
an estate in the northeast hills of Kyoto based
on the legendary retreats of scholars and poets
of the mid-T'ang dynasty of China and he
worked on this residence for over thirty years,
from 1636 until his death in 1672. Thereafter the
garden was severely neglected until 1825, when
it was rebuilt somewhat differently from the
description in Jozan's writings. The lower two
garden terraces were added after World War II.

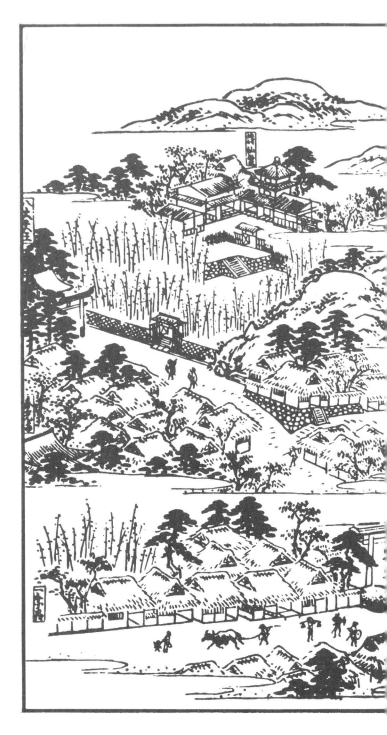

八大天王　詩仙堂　小山御坊　一乗寺村

fig. 10.1 *Late eighteenth-century wood-block print of Shisendo.*

For descriptive purposes, the compound can be divided into three main parts (Fig. 10.5): the entry garden (A), the inner garden (B), and the new garden (C). The long, secluded entry pathway passes tunnel-like through what appears to be dense forest (Fig. 10.6). This garden serves as a psychological transition from the everyday world into the rarefied atmosphere of the literati retreat.

Shisendo's three buildings have a rustic quality (thatched roofs, unhewn branches in the structure, and other details), not unlike the tea houses of the time (Fig. 10.7). Although Jozan was a tea devotee, he was known for unconventionality, advocating the use of steeped tea instead of the usual powdered variety, for instance. Similar examples of individual taste are seen in his garden.

The inner garden is separated from the entry garden by the buildings themselves; they act as the divider. This garden contains a mixture of many techniques seen previously. The southern part is a clipped hedge and stone composition on a bed of white sand with some important distinctions from earlier gardens: The plot is not rectangular, and this part of the garden is almost entirely covered by a large flowering camellia tree (Fig. 10.8). To the east of the viewing room, a shrunken landscape uses real water for its stream and features small stone bridges, a model pagoda, and a carefully clipped "forest" of plants and hedges (Figs. 10.9 and 10.10). Behind this, nestled against the enclosing hillside, are a 2 meter waterfall (Fig. 10.11) and a meticulously tended Shinto shrine. In the distance is heard the pleasant clacking sound of a water-propelled bamboo device (shishi-odoshi) meant to frighten away deer (Fig. 16.41).

The sense of descent from the old garden to the new is exaggerated because the visitor has to pass through a narrow passageway between tall clipped azaleas (Plate 16). The scene then opens to a broad lower garden containing numerous varieties of ornamental flowers, bushes, and trees—something rare for a Japanese garden but attributable to its modern construction (Fig. 10.12). A pathway of white sand leads the visitor further downward to the lowest terrace (Fig. 10.13). Shisendo's consistently downward sequence contrasts with most gardens, where visitors usually climb hillsides. The garden's lowest point sits beside the tallest trees of the adjoining hillside, and the contrast gives one the sense of descending into a deep river valley. One has, in fact, only gone down a few meters.

REMARKS

As it stands today, Shisendo encompasses the spirit of two different ages. The old Shisendo, like other gardens of the early Edo age, mixed various garden elements in an original way. As a residence, instead of monastic temple, Shisendo offered its maker an opportunity to express his own personality. In building a hermitage for the pursuit of scholarship and poetry, Jozan exemplified the renewed interest in Chinese thoughts and ideals among the aristocracy of his time.

The new garden has a completely different spirit. Whereas the original is subdued, shaded, and enclosed, the new garden has broad open spaces and bright flowers. On the whole, its design lacks cohesiveness. But because it is seen separately, it does not detract from appreciation of the original.

fig. 10.2 *Plan of Shisendo site and surroundings.*

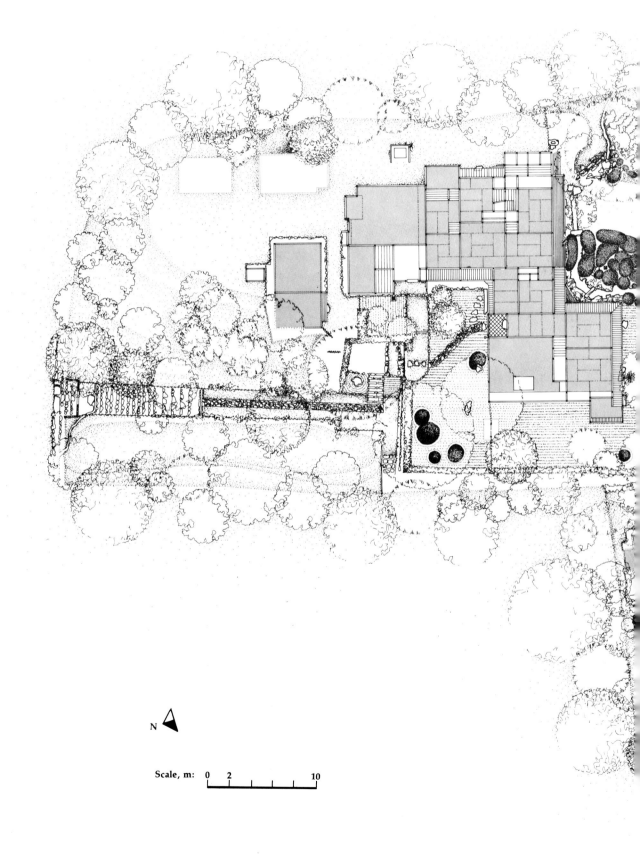

N

Scale, m: 0 2   10

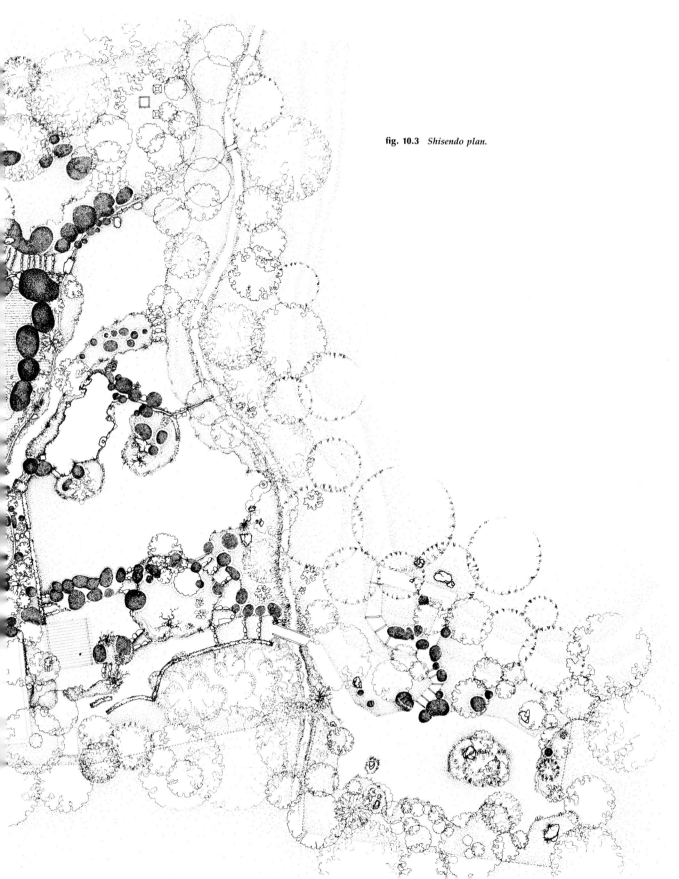

fig. 10.3 *Shisendo plan.*

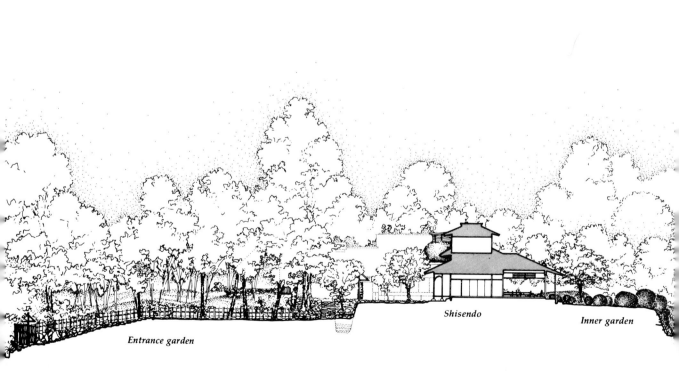

Entrance garden

Shisendo

Inner garden

fig. 10.4 *Shisendo section.*

New garden

Lower terrace of new garden

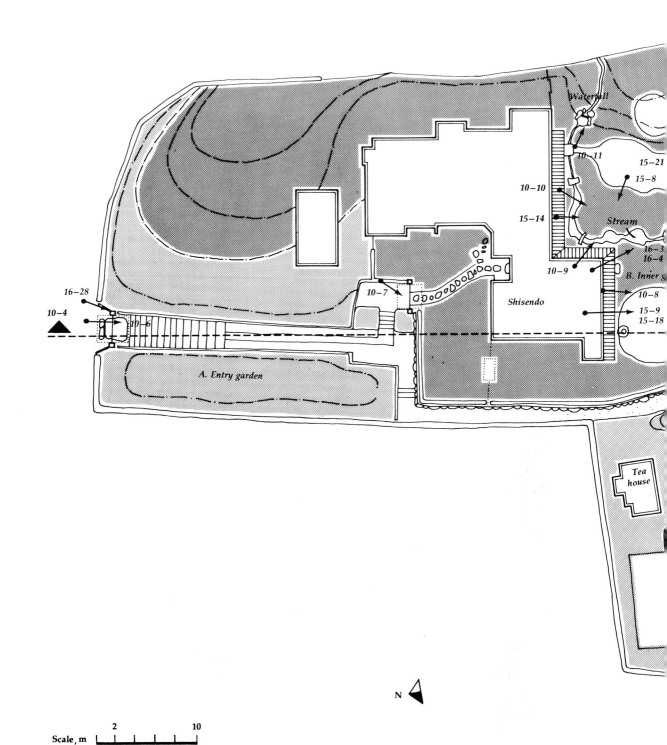

Waterfall

10–11

15–21

15–8

10–10

15–14

Stream

10–9

16–3
16–4

B. Inner 8

10–8

Shisendo

15–9
15–18

16–28

10–4

10–6

10–7

A. Entry garden

Tea
house

N

Scale, m   2   10

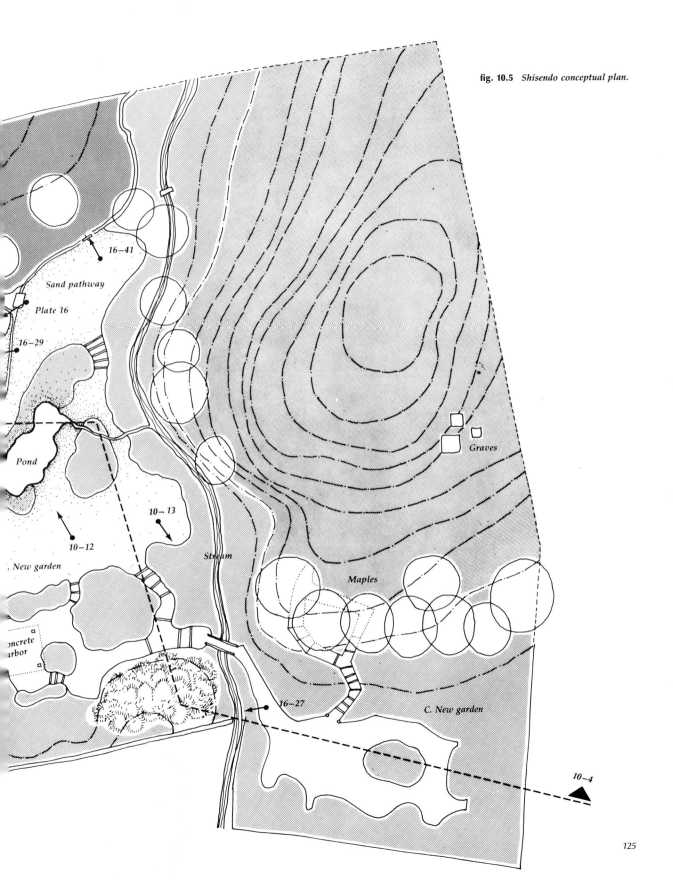

fig. 10.5 *Shisendo conceptual plan.*

16–41

Sand pathway

Plate 16

16–29

Pond

10–13

10–12

. New garden

Stream

Maples

Graves

oncrete
arbor

16–27

C. New garden

10–4

fig. 10.6 (top, left) *Entryway to Shisendo.*

fig. 10.7 (lower, left) *The inner gate of Shisendo is constructed like the buildings themselves, using materials and techniques intended to give a rustic impression.*

fig. 10.8 (top, right) *The southern part of the inner garden viewed from the Shisendo.*

fig. 10.9 (center, right) *The eastern portion of the inner garden is almost entirely filled with clipped azaleas.*

fig. 10.10 (bottom, right) *The Shisendo building looks like a garden pavilion set amid a miniature landscape.*

fig. 10.11 (top, right) *The waterfall is made in the standard way—water pours over a projecting spillway into a small pond below. Stones behind and on both sides of the fall provide an echo chamber that amplifies the sound.*

fig. 10.12 (top, left) *The broad open space of the lower garden offers a contrast to the rest of the Shisendo compound.*

fig. 10.13 (bottom) *Looking toward the lowest garden level.*

chapter eleven

Kohoan

NAME   *The name Kohoan roughly translated means the Hermitage of the Solitary Sampan.*

HISTORICAL CONTEXT AND CONTINUITY

The early Edo period (1615–1867) saw a large increase in building activity, partially as a result of renewed social stability. Kobori Enshu (1579–1647) and his family belonged to a new class of artisans employed in the design, supervision, and building of various construction projects. Enshu enjoyed a wide reputation as a builder, especially of gardens, though many works attributed to him (Katsura Villa, for example)[1] cannot actually be documented. His own residence, Kohoan, built during the later years of his life, is one verifiable example of his often imitated work. The building, originally located on a different site in Daitokuji, was moved to its present location in 1644; the garden was completed four years later. This original building and parts of the garden were destroyed by fire in the 1790s, but they were almost immediately rebuilt by Matsudaira Fumai (1758–1829), a famous feudal lord and tea ceremony devotee. Although somewhat altered in reconstruction, they are still believed to convey the spirit of Enshu's original design.

GENERAL DESCRIPTION

Kohoan can be broken down into five distinct areas (Fig. 11.4): The largest is the entry and side gardens (660 square meters); the garden in front of the main religious buildings, the *hojo*, measures 396 square meters; there are two tea gardens, one for the *bosen* room (412.5 square meters) and one for the cloud viewing platform (69 square meters); finally, there is a small interior garden (16 square meters).

The entry gardens, least damaged by the fire of 1794, contain many famous Enshu details, the entrance bridge (Fig. 16.8) and the pathway (Figs. 11.5, 16.14, and 16.37) in particular. The side gardens feature some clipped hedges and cut stones for hand washing (Fig. 15.22).

The *hojo* garden has a rectangular format and southern orientation typical of Zen gardens. The ground is covered with moss and pine needles, and the enclosure is formed by two clipped hedges, also something of an Enshu trademark (Fig. 11.6). Originally this garden incorporated a borrowed scenery view of the "shiplike shape" of Mt. Funaoka, but the full-grown trees now obscure this.

The garden of the *bosen* room is meant to give one the impression of being on a boat (Fig. 11.7). Kohoan is the "solitary sampan," and *bosen* refers to a Zen proverb about fishing.[2] The imagery of this garden is said to be based on a famous Chinese landscape painting theme of the "Eight Views of the River Hsiang" (Fig. 11.8), and all the special features of the *bosen* room—the always open doorway to the garden, the veranda, and the balustrade—attempt to give a boatlike impression (Plate 18). In the garden itself we see a condensed landscape, where pine needles which cover the moss in winter serve as the water surface and many features—such as a dry waterfall, stone bridges, and lanterns—contribute to this impression (Figs. 11.9, 11.10, and 16.7).

The smaller tea garden of the cloud viewing pavilion is mainly noted for its tea ceremony artifacts, the hand-washing basin, and the lantern (Fig. 11.11).

REMARKS

Kohoan was built at a time when members of the tea cult had become the final arbitrators of taste. Enshu's garden marks a high point in representing their values: It demonstrates refined literary allusions and Zen art forms in a sophisticated, integrated manner. Although it claims to be a humble hermitage, Kohoan was designed to be and remains today a standard of Japanese elegance.

NOTES

[1] See Kenzo Tange and Walter Gropius, *Katsura: Tradition and Creation in Japanese Architecture*, Yale, New Haven, 1960.

[2] "To catch the fish and forget the net," as the proverb goes, alludes to the loss of self-consciousness in action that is the aspiration of Zen devotees.

ADDITIONAL NOTES TO PART ONE

The historical accounts of the gardens in Part One are based mainly on Mirei Shigemori, *Nihon Teien Shi Zukan (Illustrated History of Japanese Gardens)*, 26 vols., Yukosha, Tokyo, 1936–1939. The plans are based on his drawings which have been redrawn, updated, and occasionally expanded.

The wood-block prints of the gardens come from *Miyako Meisho Zue (Pictures of Famous Places in the Capital)*, 7 vols., 1781–1787.

Other works consulted are:

Ken Domon and Seishi Yamaguchi, *Nihon no Tera: Saihoji, Ryoanji (Japanese Temples: Saihoji, Ryoanji)*, Bijitsu Shupansha, Tokyo, 1959.
Masao Hayakawa, *The Garden Art of Japan*, Weatherhill/Heibonsha, Tokyo, 1973.
Teiji Itoh, *Space and Illusion in the Japanese Garden*, Weatherhill/Tankosha, Tokyo 1965.
Loraine Kuck, *The World of the Japanese Garden*, Walker/Weatherhill, Tokyo, 1968.
Osamu Mori, *Nippon no Niwa (Japanese Gardens)*, with English summary, Asahi Shibun Shupansha, Tokyo, 1960.
Osamu Mori, *Typical Japanese Gardens*, Shibata/Japan Publications, Tokyo, 1962.
Kinsaku Nakane, *Kyoto Gardens*, Hoikusha, Osaka, 1965.
Masaru Sekino, ed., *Nihon no Bijitsu 2, No. 153: Kinkaku to Ginkaku*, (Arts of Japan 2, No. 153: Kinkaku and Ginkaku), Shibundo, Tokyo, 1979.
Yoshinobu Yoshinaga, *Nihon no Teien* (Japanese Traditional Gardens, English and Japanese), Shokokusha, Tokyo, 1962.

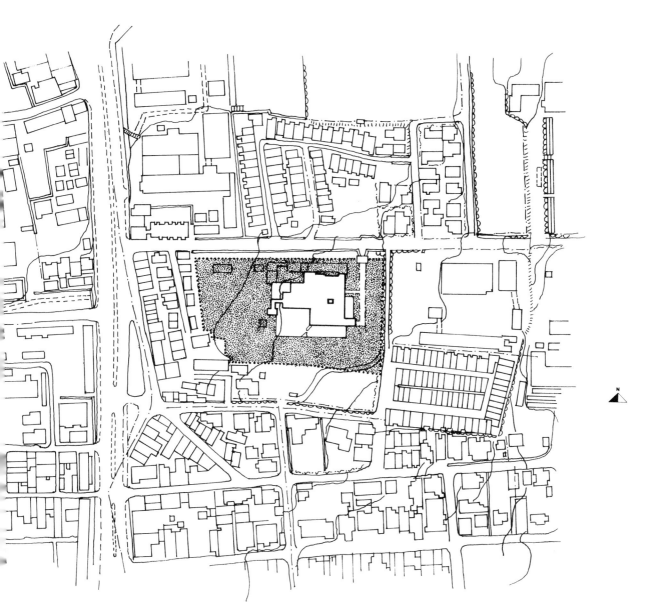

fig. 11.1 *Plan of Kohoan site and surroundings*

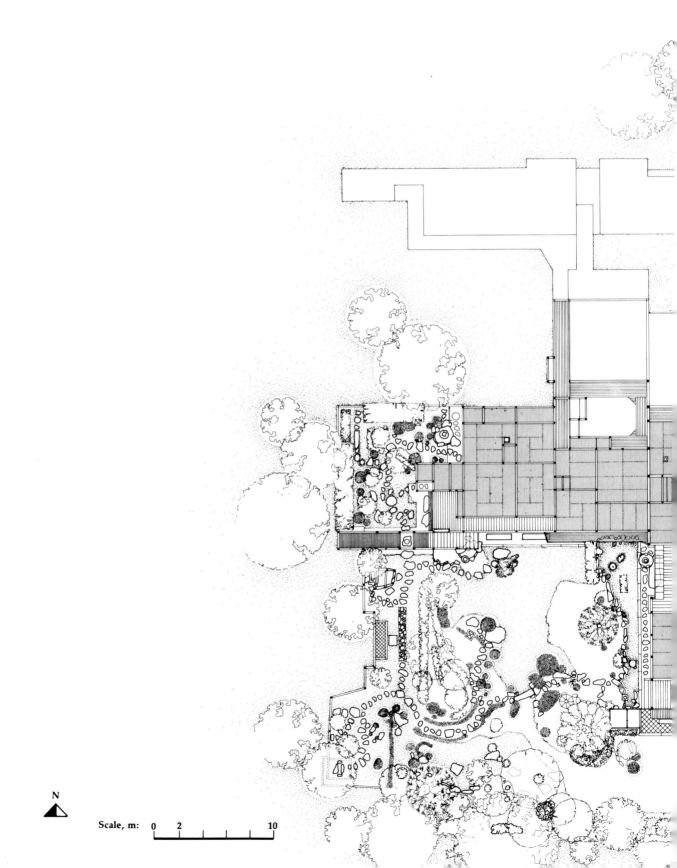

N

Scale, m: 0   2   10

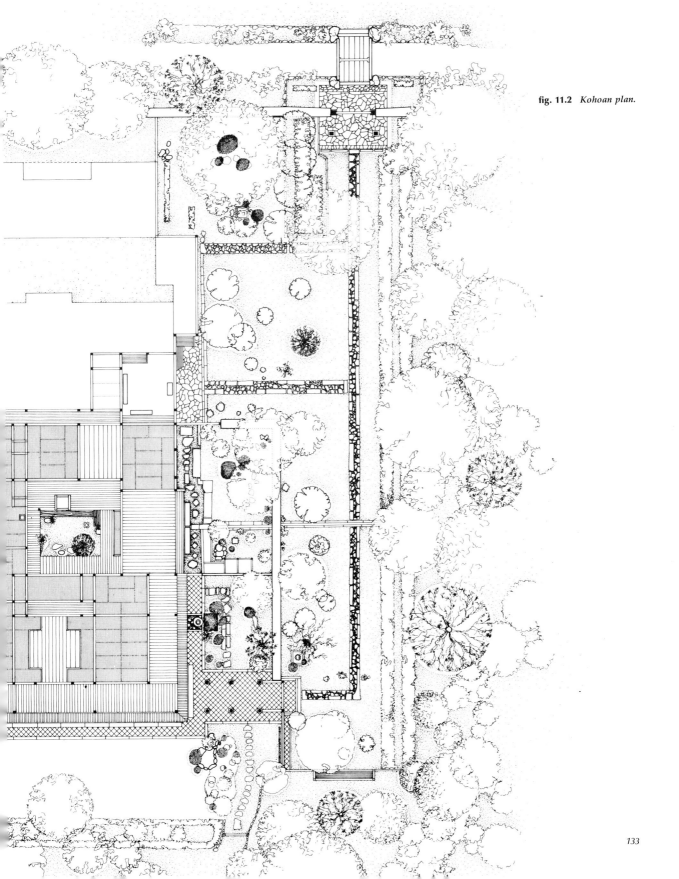

fig. 11.2 *Kohoan plan.*

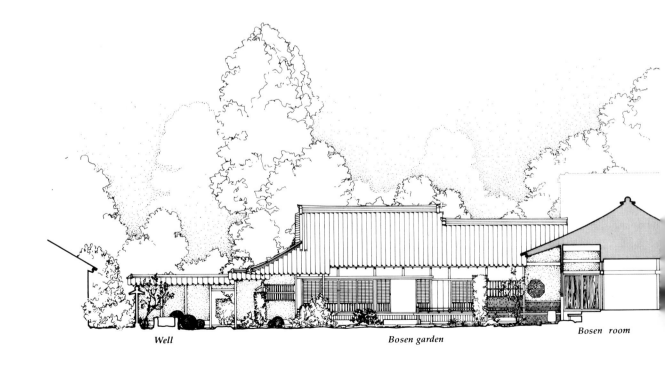

Well   Bosen garden   Bosen room

fig. 11.3 *Kohoan section.*

Interior garden   Side garden   Entry garden

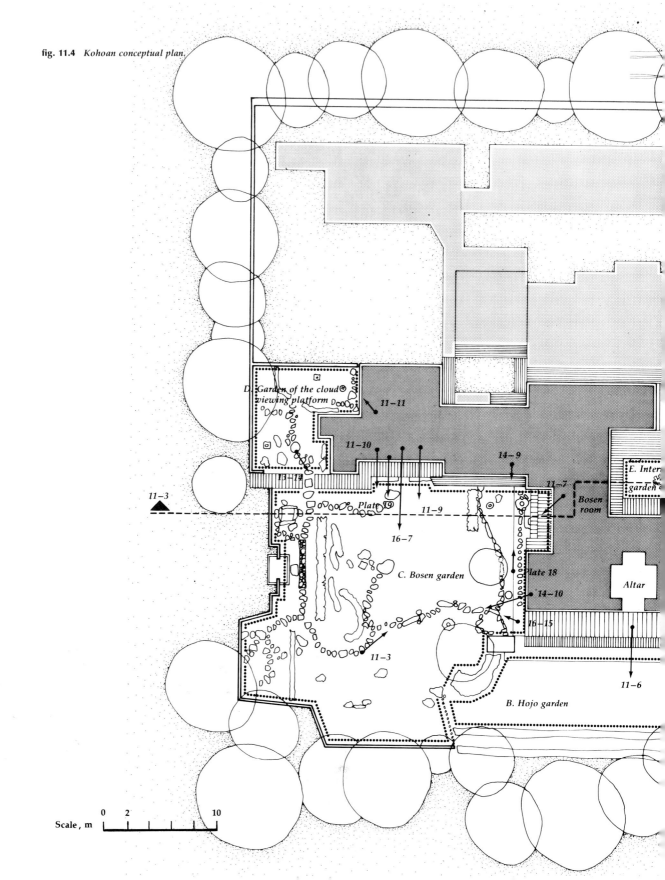

fig. 11.4 *Kohoan conceptual plan.*

D. Garden of the cloud®
viewing platform

11–11

11–10

14–9

E. Inter
garden

Bosen
room

11–7

11–3

Plate 19

11–9

16–7

C. Bosen garden

Plate 18

14–10

11–3

16–15

Altar

11–6

B. Hojo garden

Scale , m

0   2   10

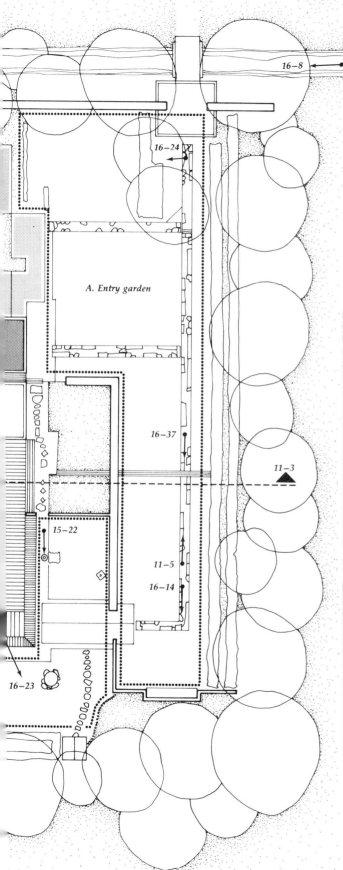

16–8

16–24

A. Entry garden

16–37

11–3

15–22

11–5

16–14

16–23

fig. 11.5 (left) *Entryway to Kohoan.*

fig. 11.6 (below) *The hojo garden is enclosed by a double hedge. Pine needles are used to protect the moss ground cover in winter.*

OPPOSITE PAGE:

fig. 11.7 (bottom, left) *The bottom portion of the wall is always open, allowing a continual view of the garden, as if from the deck of a boat. The pebbles are meant to symbolize the seacoast.*

fig. 11.8 (top) *Detail of* Returning Sails off the Distant Coast, *one of the "Eight Views of the River Hsiang" that form the theme of the* bosen *garden. This particular painting was once owned by Matsudaira Fumai, who restored the garden in the late eighteenth century. (Collection of Mrs. Sen Hinohara.)*

fig. 11.9 (bottom, right) *The foreground symbolizes the river's surface.*

THIS PAGE:

fig. 11.10 (top, left) *The dwarf pine in the foreground increases the sense of depth.*

fig. 11.11 (bottom) *View of the cloud viewing platform garden. Its western orientation, like that of the* bosen *room, requires hanging sunshades.*

fig. 11.12 (top, right) *The buildings of Kohoan seen from the garden.*

part two

The Sources

chapter twelve

Japanese Traditions

THE LANDSCAPE

Much of what is considered unique to Japan is in some part related to geography. As a nation of islands, Japan avoided invasion, developed an original homogeneous culture, and was even able to seal itself off from the rest of the world for over two centuries. The island landscape of Japan suggested many of the scenes found in Japanese gardens, as some gardeners sought to replicate in miniature the seascapes, coastal plains, and mountains that are familiar sights of the countryside.

The land offers neither abruptly dramatic scenery nor much in mineral wealth. Roughly four-fifths of the land consists of low, rolling mountains covered by luxuriant evergreen forests that are supplied with water year round by numerous fast-running streams. These streams have cut out river valleys whose broader stretches contain terraced rice paddies and small villages. The lower hills are often planted with fruit trees, while the upper regions are forested for timber. Today the entire country seems to be under cultivation in one way or another. The mountains look like tapestries with various shades of green showing the different groves. These mountainous interior regions today, as before, remain relatively difficult to reach (Fig. 12.1).

The first real cities of Japan developed along the coastal regions of the Inland Sea (Fig. 1.4). Here, sheltered from the Siberian winter winds by the northern mountains and from the fall typhoons by the southern islands, this region enjoys a temperate climate with generous rainfall. Nor is it as seismically active as the land to the northeast, where Tokyo was constructed during the later centuries. The Inland Sea's calm, protected water was the principal artery for both domestic and foreign communication. Taking the water route was easier and faster than trying to negotiate the winding mountain paths. Across the narrow straits at the west end of the Inland Sea lay Korea, and from there Japan first learned about the higher arts of civilization. People of prominence were frequent travelers, even going as far as China from the seventh century onward. Their familiarity with seascapes is one reason for the popularity of water scenes in gardens (Fig. 12.2).

fig. 12.1 (upper) *Set in a valley just beyond the hills of northern Kyoto, the village of Hanase—like many other hamlets in the area—is relatively untouched by modern environmental changes.*

fig. 12.2 (lower) *Coastal scenes like this must have served as inspiration for generations of garden makers.*

The alluvial plains along the coast also offered adequate flat land for both agricultural cultivation and urbanization. The first capital cities of Asuka, Nara, and Kyoto were all built here, protected by sheltering hills that seemed to give the landscape a human sense of scale. In these urban compounds, situated in the most ideal of locations, the first gardens were built.

The benevolence of the Japanese physical surroundings can be best illustrated by comparison with the environment of the less fortunate Chinese. Alexander Soper, a leading authority on Chinese and Japanese architectural history, describes it thus:

The ancient China of the Yellow River region is a land at once vast and pitiless. The bleak, dusty plains are without end, the mountains terrible in their height and bareness; the great wild river rolls from its unimaginable source into the world of men, wide, swift, and irresistible; periodically, as if by intentional malice, it changes its course to the sea, and whole countries are obliterated. Summer is a time of fiery heat, winter of bitter cold; spring brings incessant winds from the Gobi desert, laden with a biting dust; every few years, again, as if by caprice, the rain fails, there is a period of drought, and thousands are driven from their homes or die of starvation. A Nature so immense and inhuman must either crush its inhabitants into fatalism or rouse them to some sort of defiance.[1]

The land of Japan prompted an entirely different response from its inhabitants. Everything about the landscape—its scale, form, and climate—seemed moderate and sympathetic to the ways of humans. The earliest Japanese poetry speaks with praise and gratitude about the homeland. People developed a deep sense of appreciation for the beauty of their land, which has been a continuing source of inspiration for artists and craftsmen. The Japanese sensibilities in design are in no small way dependent on this special relationship with nature. For the garden artist, in particular, the landscape was the greatest teacher.

THE INDIGENOUS CULT: THE SHINTO FAITH

The early Japanese recognized more than beauty in the landscape: They also saw it richly populated with spirits. Mostly benign, but in need of human attention and courtesies, these spirits called *kami* inhabited almost any natural object, including mountains, stones, rivers, and trees, or hovered in the sky. Aspects of ancestor worship were later amalgamated into this tradition, which has partically no written body of thought and not much plastic art. But as a variety of nature worship, it deeply affected the way garden makers looked at both the land and their materials and also affected the viewer's perception of the finished garden.

In the early stages of the cult, spirits were summoned down to earth by a special ritual into a sacred compound. This compound was usually a small rectangular clearing in the forest that was ritually purified so a spirit could enter without being defiled. The plot of ground was covered with pebbles of uniform color and enclosed by a holy straw rope or fence to distinguish its sacredness from the profane surroundings. The compound was usually bare except for a single sacred tree, the *sakaki* (Cleyera japonica), through which the priests would invite the spirit to enter the hallowed ground. The sacred compound can be considered the earliest form of Japanese gardens, as its name *saniwa* (sand garden) indicates.[2] The pebble ground covering, the rectangular plot, and the fenced enclosure are characteristic of shrines found throughout Japan today (Fig. 12.3).

fig. 12.3 *The purified ground of the Ise Outer Shrine is covered with white and gray pebbles.*

Spirits were also thought to take up residence of their own accord in some natural object. Anything outwardly unusual in size or form was thought to indicate the presence of a *kami* dwelling within. Unusual trees and stones were wrapped with holy straw ropes to signify their sacredness[3] (Fig. 12.4). Small buildings were sometimes erected to protect and house the *kami* or sacred swords, mirrors, and jewels. It is very rare for even the highest priests to see these sacred objects: Nature is deeply felt to be mysterious and incomprehensible. Rituals and architecture reinforced this concept by imposing many veils of mystery between the worshiper and the object of reverence (Fig. 12.5).

Worship of mountains played a central role in the cult. They were seen as the dwelling places of both *kami* and the benign and honored dead. In the countryside, a sacred mountain is recognized by its conical shape or especially lush vegetation (Fig. 12.6). Mt. Fuji is the most famous sacred mountain, but there are many others, some of which are still taboo for women to climb. Such mountains are the sacred domain of the gods and are therefore purified; women are prohibited because menstrual blood is considered a severe form of pollution. Even a mountain that is not conical may contain a myriad of *kami* and is usually covered with small shrine buildings.

fig. 12.4 *An enshrined stone at Kamigamo Shrine, Kyoto. The stone is wrapped with a* **Shimenawa** *(sacred rope) and protected by a permanent shelter. The vessels and flowers in front are offerings to the* **kami** *within.*

fig. 12.5 (upper) *Ordinarily people are not permitted to enter the inner precincts of Kamigamo Shrine. The sacred object is kept behind closed doors that lie beyond the cloth veils in the entryway. See also Fig. 12.10, which illustrates the successive layer of fences surrounding the Ise Shrine.*

fig. 12.6 (lower) *The sand cone of Ginkakuji is patterned after the sacred volcanic mountains found throughout Japan. During the Edo period, when this feature was added to the garden, the conical shape of Mt. Fuji near Tokyo was a popular art motif.*

To ensure a secure dwelling for their souls, and to make the passage between heaven and earth easier, emperors of the Prehistoric Age constructed large artificial mountains as tombs. These keyhole-shaped earthworks were the largest examples of civil architecture in pre-Buddhist Japan[4] (Fig. 12.7). In succeeding ages, small artificial mountains were also constructed in gardens and shrine buildings were invariably placed upon them (Fig. 12.8). These small buildings, reminiscent of the ones found in the "real" landscape, are themselves actual shrines erected for the benefit of the original *kami* that inhabited the garden site, or for some particularly famous personage associated with its history.

On a smaller scale, stones were seen as favorite vessels for *kami*. Stones are believed to be hollow and actually to grow as the inhabiting *kami* swells during the ages. The Japanese national anthem, referring to the Emperor, says, "May your reign last for thousands of years until the pebbles turn into moss covered rocks."[5] In addition, these stone *kami* have personality. Even today, gardeners talk to stones, trying to soothe or coax the spirit inside so that it will cooperate and participate in the garden. Stones are also fertility symbols, most often because of their phallic shape, though they can be feminine. Phallic worship was, and still is, an important component of the cult.[6] A garden maker had thus to consider the disposition (hostile or friendly), influence (powerful or weak), and even the gender of the stones when planning the garden arrangements. Works of common people seen throughout the countryside demonstrate this concern for the well-being of stones (Fig. 12.9).

fig. 12.7 (left)   Tomb of the Emperor Nintoku, fifth century, near Osaka. The enormous keyhole-shaped mound is surrounded by moats.

fig. 12.8 (upper)   Artificial mountain and shrine building in Ginkakuji.

fig. 12.9 (lower)   The two stones are "married" by the sacred rope joining them. Futami village in Mie prefecture near the Ise Shrine.

Scale: |_____|_____|_____|
              100 m

Assurance of fertility was essential to the agrarian Japanese and was a major objective of religious practices. Life and growth were seen as good; death and decay were seen as bad. Any indication of decay had to be removed lest it "infect" the living and the spiritual, and many rituals developed to cleanse people of all impurities. Some of these practices have filtered down to the present and are recognizable features of gardening elements. Before entering a shrine, for example, people wash their hands and rinse their mouths with water. The tea ceremony has a similar preparatory ritual; gardens built for tea ceremony always include a stylized water basin for this purpose. Salt is spread around an area to remove impurities, especially when there is a death, and the white sand cones at Daisen-in (Figs. 6.9 and 13.2) remind us of the smaller salt cones placed in front of homes and shrines for purification.

The foulest sources of pollution are blood and death. Anyone who has direct contact with the sick, the wounded, or a corpse must undergo rites of purification. The death taboo had a retarding influence on the development of early Japanese architecture. As soon as an emperor died, his palace—indeed, his entire capital—was abandoned, for anything touched by the corpse had been defiled. Thus, in pre-Buddhist times, Japanese architecture was always regarded as temporary: The "palaces" were little more than huts made entirely from vegetable materials. Even the great shrine at Ise was not considered an enduring building but one that required total rebuilding every twenty years[7] (Fig. 12.10).

The introduction of Chinese learning and Buddhism eventually changed some of these practices. After Buddhism was established as the state religion (seventh century), the construction of large burial tombs was prohibited. Time and labor that had gone into their making was redirected into building temples which employed the relatively advanced construction technology learned from China and Korea. The increasing scale of these projects, the introduction of ceramic building materials, and the relaxation of the death taboo as a result of Buddhist teaching favored the acceptance of a more permanent architecture.

As Buddhism now introduced a point of

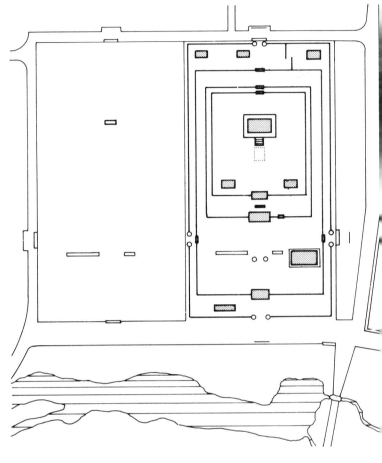

comparison, a word had to be coined for the previously unnamed set of indigenous rituals and beliefs. The word Shinto comes from the Chinese *Shentao*, which means the mystic rules of nature and/or the path leading to a grave.[8] The Buddhists did not try to eliminate the existing Shinto but instead assimilated it. Over the centuries, deities, art, and architecture from the two religions have blended, but there still remains a distinction. Japanese often consider themselves to be members of both faiths, which explains the apparent paradox of finding Shinto shrines within Buddhist gardens. The expression that a Japanese is born Shinto and dies Buddhist refers to Shinto's continuing sphere of influence in rituals of fertility, marriage ceremonies, and christenings and to

Buddhism's province of the other world after death.

One can't help but feel that part of the Japanese skill in craftsmanship and quality in design is related to the Shinto belief that all material is inhabited by some kind of spirit. Thus the craftsman empathizes with materials and treats them with reverence and respect. A good example is the kimono, the traditional Japanese dress, which is made only from uncut pieces of material because cutting the cloth would injure the *kami* inside.[9] The patience, precision, and concern of a Japanese gardener demonstrates the same kind of respect for materials.

NOTES

[1]Alexander C. Soper, *The Evolution of Buddhist Architecture in Japan*, Princeton University Press, 1942, p. 14.

[2]Carmen Blacker, *The Catalpa Bow: A Study of Shamanistic Practice in Japan*, G. Allen, London, 1975, p. 108.

[3]For a discussion of these ritual ropes see Günter Nitschke, "Shime Binding/Unbinding," *Architectural Design*, December 1974.

[4]J. E. Kidder, *Japan Before Buddhism*, Thames & Hudson, London, 1959, pp. 145–160.

[5]Blacker, op. cit., p. 99.

[6]See Michael Czaja, *Gods of Myth and Stone: Phallicism in Japanese Folk Religion*, Weatherhill, Tokyo, 1974.

[7]See Yasutada Watanabe, *Shinto Art: Ise and Izumo Shrines*, Weatherhill/Heibonsha, Tokyo, 1974.

[8]John P. Kouletsis, "The Development of a Residential Architecture in Japan: Shoin Zukuri," unpublished thesis, Kyoto University, 1978, p. 20.

[9]Haruiki Kageyama, *The Arts of Shinto*, Arts of Japan, vol. 4, Shibundo/Weatherhill, Tokyo, 1973, p. 9.

fig. 12.10 *The plan of Ise shows the two alternate sites for the sacred buildings. Every twenty years, an identical new building is erected on the vacant site and the old one dismantled. The ground of the unused site (left) is covered with white pebbles such as those seen in fig. 12.3.*

chapter thirteen

Chinese Influences

By the time Chinese teachings reached Japan in earnest in the sixth century, the Chinese had already developed a comprehensive and sophisticated understanding of the physical universe. To the literate Chinese, who had developed knowledge in the areas of astronomy, mathmatics, civil engineering, and other fields, the landscape had meanings beyond the animistic sacredness attributed to it by the Japanese. In landscape the Chinese saw the working of great universal forces and laws. Observation of nature not only provided spiritual inspiration but offered a key to cosmic understanding.

Unlike the Japanese of the time, the Chinese were great builders, and their cities, temples, tombs, and homes were modeled after their conceptions of the universal order. In addition, the arts of landscape gardening and painting were meant to exemplify the action of cosmic design.

LANDSCAPE PHILOSOPHY: THE HARMONIC IDEAL

Certain Ideas run like main currents throughout the course of Chinese philosophy. There is a central assumption that the universe is in constant change, a continuing process of growth and decay, creation and destruction, life and death. Everything is subject to this process, and nothing remains static: Just as the clouds change shape in the wind and the stars move in the heavens, so too do the mountains and valleys change, though they move too slowly for human observation. Two great opposing forces are revealed in this constant process, and since time immemorial they have been called yin and yang.

Yin is female, mother, negative, dark, damp, deep, and destructive. Yang is male, father, positive, bright, hard, high, penetrating, and constructive. Between these opposite poles, the great oscillations of the universe take place. Neither can exist independently, for all things yang contain some small element of yin and vice versa. In the extreme of one we see the creation of the other in a pattern much like a sinusoidal wave: Strong activity results in rest, as extreme winter coldness gives way to spring warmth. Thus creation is seen as a multitude of cyclic processes represented by black-and-white diagrams that express these whirling patterns of change (Figs. 13.1, and 13.2).

fig. 13.1 (upper) *A Chinese dish of the tenth century with a design representing the ebb and flow of the great forces. (Victoria and Albert Museum, London, diameter twenty-six centimeters.)*

fig. 13.2 (lower) *The snow-capped sand cone at Daisen-in forms a pattern reminiscent of the yin-yang design.*

fig. 13.3 (opposite, left) *The hand-washing stone at Ryoanji is in the form of traditional Chinese and Japanese coins.*

fig. 13.4 (opposite, right) *The hermit retreat as pictured by the Chinese artist Sun Chun-tse, Yuan Dynasty (1208–1368). (Private collection, Japan.)*

A goal in life, as well as in art, for many was to achieve harmony: harmony of forces within an individual and of those without. Internally, various practices (yoga) were used to manipulate and balance breathing and sexual energy, which were considered direct human manifestations of yin and yang forces. Externally, people sought to integrate their homes and ancestral tombs with the energy in the environment. Landscape was invested with sexual attributes, and every element could be classified, depending on shape and quality, into yin or yang. The very word for landscape, a combination of the Chinese characters for mountain (yang) and water (yin), implies this dualism. Landscape art, both painting and gardening, sought to represent ideal harmony. The "opening and closing" relationships of hills and valleys, positive and negative shapes, horizontal and vertical, were invoked as evidence of balanced yin and yang.

Other symbols were also used to express the workings of yin and yang. A primary idea of Chinese culture was the division of the universe into three parts: heaven, earth, and man. The problems of human existence could be solved by reconciling the claims of heaven (yang) and earth (yin). Heaven, represented by a circle, was seen as the source of the various energies that worked through the passive earth (represented by a square) where people labored to effect favorable changes for themselves in their present life and after death. The old-fashioned Chinese coin—a circle pierced by a square with an Imperial inscription between the two forms—represents this fundamental relationship (Fig. 13.3). A chief function of the Emperor was to serve as an intermediary between the two realms.[1] By performing rites in his palace and city, which were specifically designed for this purpose, he attempted to reconcile the claims of each. A major natural diaster was an almost certain sign that the Emperor was unsuccessful in fulfilling his duties.

Chinese landscape art always depicted elements of heaven, earth, and people, or something man-made (such as a path or bridge), implying that no matter how small the human element seemed in comparison to the majestic mountains and seas, the scene was not complete without some indication of human presence. Landscape painting tried to show the harmonic ideal, and great engineering feats—which imply the subjugation of nature—are usually not pictured. Conversely, ruins or wrecks such as those painted in romantic European landscapes, suggesting the domination of nature over people, never appear in East Asian landscape paintings.

Such paintings instead pictured a person in complete harmony with the environment: hence the recurring figure in painting and literature of the scholar hermit in his retreat. Freed from the petty concerns and intrigues of an official career, the hermit scholar was able to find inspiration, insight, and fulfillment amid the mountains and rivers of the countryside. Most often pictured alone—or with a single attendant—living in a simple thatched hut, the recluse represented an ultimate in tranquillity and harmony[2] (Fig. 13.4).

This ideal image had a lasting impact on garden form in Japan. Indeed, later on this was a principal reason for building a garden in the first place. As the Japanese tried to recreate the setting of a retreat amid the "wildness" of nature, architecture and landscape gardening were designed to meet this purpose. Even the most elaborate Japanese structures were little more than pavilions, easily opened to the garden outside, while the humble ceremonial tea house of the Japanese tea garden takes its form directly from the hut of a retreat (Fig. 13.5). The buildings and the garden surroundings attempted to recreate this ideal, which reflected the harmony and balance of the cosmos.

fig. 13.5 (above) *The tea house at Kinkakuji, early seventeenth century.*

fig. 13.6 (opposite, top) *A relatively late Chinese depiction of the inner human body rendered in landscape forms, rubbing dated 1886. (Private collection.)*

fig. 13.7 (opposite, bottom) *The fully developed geomantic compass contains twenty-four concentric rings for evaluating site conditions and the positions of the heavenly bodies. (Whipple Museum, Cambridge.) See Feuchtwang,[12] for a full description of its use.*

LANDSCAPE PRACTICE: GEOMANCY

Given this expressed goal of harmony, these questions must be asked: How did the Chinese, and later the Japanese, conceive of nature (heaven and earth) and how did they try to harmonize with it when building cities, homes, and gardens? Analysis of Chinese geomancy provides answers to both questions in summary form. Defined as "the art of adapting the residences of the living and the dead so as to cooperate and harmonize with the local currents of the cosmic breath,"[3] geomancy has been the subject of considerable interest and controversy. Ernest Eitel,[4] writing in 1873, called geomancy *(feng-shui,* Chinese, and *fusui,* Japanese—literally meaning wind and water) the "rudiments of Chinese natural science," and he recorded the strong objections voiced by the Chinese of Hong Kong to British planned improvements such as telegraphs, railroads, and even church spires because they violated geomantic principles. Joseph Needham called geomancy a "far reaching pseudo science" and acknowledged its contributions to modern science, such as the invention of the magnetic compass (Fig. 13.7) and the attention to landscape that resulted in topographical mapping[5] (Fig. 13.10). Loraine Kuck[6] in her study of Japanese gardens ignored geomancy completely, believing it had misled Josiah Conder[7] in his first explanations of the gardens; but she recognized the role it played in the "secret" manual of Japanese gardeners. It is now thought to be a principal foundation of urban planning in the Chinese realm[8] with geomantic ideas closely incorporated into early garden making practice.

The concern of geomancy for integrating structures of human origin with the great forces of nature made it the "ecology" of its day. The "wind and waters" of Chinese geomancy refer to the cosmic breath or energy *(ch'i)* of heaven and earth, which had to be determined for a particular site before anything could be built. Earth here means the living biological earth where seasonal cycles of plant and animal life seemed to demonstrate the fixed mathematical laws seen in the motions of the heavenly bodies. The fundamental energy of *ch'i,* which flows through the heavens, was similarly perceived to be flowing through the bodies of all living things, including the "body" of earth (Fig. 13.6). Just as humans have veins and acupuncture sites where *ch'i* can be stimulated and adjusted, the earth too had veins (surface

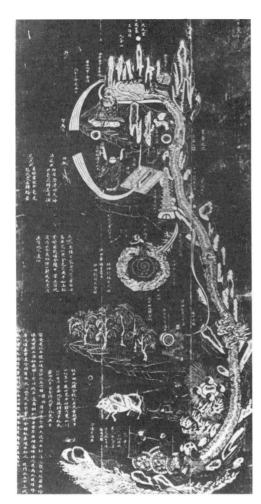

be fragrant and flourishing; and all men and things will be pure and wise . . . but if the ch'i of the earth is stopped up, then the water and earth and natural products will be bitter, cold and withered . . . and all men and things will be evil and foolish.[10]

This relationship between people and the earth was considered very delicate and easily damaged or repaired:

When Hideyoshi's [d. 1598] soldiers of Japan invaded Korea, they set up camp in Sonsan for a time. A Japanese geomancer of the army unit observed the form of the mountains and realized that the place would produce many great men and that Korea would be prosperous.

For this reason, the Japanese geomancer advised the soldiers to burn an important place on the mountain in the back of Sonsan town and to drive in a great iron piling. In this way he killed the vital energy for the mountain.

After that time, strangely, no great men were born in Sonsan or even in the neighbouring counties.

Thus, until a few decades ago it is said that people were roaming around in the mountains of Sonsan County in order to find the iron bar.[11]

The key factor affecting the energy of a site was its orientation, and the magnetic compass was first developed in service to geomancy. It was used by the Chinese for site reading and planning centuries before they used it for navigation (Fig. 13.7). The original compass consisted of a square plate (representing the

and subterranean watercourses) and centers of ch'i. This is graphically described by a fourteenth-century Chinese scientist:

The body of the earth is like that of a human being. . . . Ordinary people, not being able to see the veins and vessels which are disposed in order within the body of man, think that it is no more than a lump of solid flesh. Likewise, not being able to see the veins and vessels which are disposed in order under the ground, they think that the earth is just a homogeneous mass.[9]

Just as a person should be judged for signs of sickness or health by physical appearance, so could a prospective building site. This was extremely important, for the health of human beings was seen to be directly interrelated with the health of their environment:

Now if the ch'i of the earth can get through the veins, then the water and the earth above will

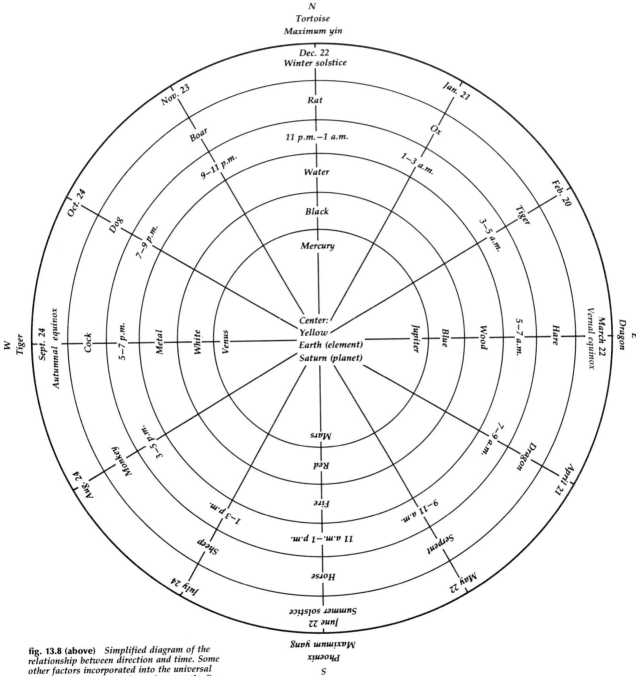

fig. 13.8 (above) *Simplified diagram of the relationship between direction and time. Some other factors incorporated into the universal scheme of the compass shown here are the five planets, the five elements, the five colors, and the twelve symbolic animals.*

fig. 13.9 (opposite) *The geomancer consulting his compass when selecting a city site. This nineteenth-century print was used anachronistically to illustrate a much older text (after Needham, vol. 2).*

earth) marked with the main compass points beneath a polished circular disk (representing heaven); a magnetic spoon made from lodestone modeled after the shape of the Big Dipper was placed on the disk to indicate direction. Subsequent developments saw the spoon replaced by the familiar dry pivot compass, which was surrounded by numerous concentric rings pertaining to both the positions of the heavens and the conditions of the landscape. One ring, for example, is based on the twelve-year cycle of Jupiter, with each year represented by an animal. On the compass dial, each of the twelve divisions also pertains to a month, a direction, and a two-hour period of the day (Fig. 13.8). Time and direction were thus inseparably linked in the Chinese classification, and the compass, like the calendar year, was divided into 365¼ units. The geomantic compass embodied large portions of the Chinese understanding of natural processes.[12]

In building site selection, ideally the geomancer would be free to choose the most auspicious spot in the landscape. Often, however, such selection was not possible and, in these cases, the geomancer was called upon to evaluate and provide instructions for site improvements (Fig. 13.9). The compass was aligned and calculations were made regarding positions of the heavens. Next, important landscape features were observed and their relative position noted. A tally was kept of all these important celestial and terrestrial factors, and the final computations resulted in a formula for building: Perhaps a pond had to be dug or an artificial mountain built; a too-yang angular hill might have to be rounded by bushes or a too-yin site might need some prominent trees or stones. Like a giant acupuncture needle, a pagoda might be erected to stimulate the local currents of ch'i.

When reading the actual landscape, geomancers found significance in many things. Mountains, often called "dragons" in the geomantic literature, were the most powerful determinants of ch'i. In general, geomancers sought to avoid disturbing the sleeping dragons. Just before his death, a builder of the Great Wall remarked, "I could not make the Great Wall without cutting through the veins of the earth."[13] Stones (and dinosaur bones) were often called the bones of the dragons and were considered to harbor great concentrations of energy.

The origin and flow of watercourses was next in importance in determining the ch'i of a site. Water could block the flow of ch'i and thus could be harmful if it prevented ch'i from entering a site, or good if it helped concentrate the ch'i by slowing its exit. Underground watercourses were also carefully noted, as were wind and soil conditions.

This attention to natural phenomena resulted in some practical benefits. The first thing recommended by a geomancer was a south-facing site, preferably protected by a horseshoe-shaped mountain closed on all sides

except the south. In terms of sun exposure and protection from bad weather, this makes sound sense environmentally, as does the predilection for flowing water near dwellings. Geomantic practice placed the dwelling in the "belly of the dragon," i.e:, inside the bend of a river, where it was not prone to the eroding action that cuts away the outside bank (Fig. 13.10). A strong aversion to underground seepage led to careful observation of terrain and soil, which was examined for "inauspicious" insects at the same time. This careful site selection was practical, as was the planting of trees to form a windbreak in accord with the geomantic preference for a calm site. Trees were also often planted simply to balance the energy of a site.

A large part of geomancy—its less functional side—was concerned with allegorical readings of meaning in the landscape. Land forms were given descriptive poetic names such as the "sitting general" or "horses standing still," and the needs and functions of landscape were assessed in allegorical terms as illustrated by this story from Korea, where Chinese geomancy was also practiced:

The Kim family of Sangchon lived in Mokchon village with great prosperity and power. Whenever a new governor of Andong County arrived, he had to visit the family first and greet them. When Maeng Sasong came to Andong as the governor of the county, he thought that this visit was not the right thing to do for a person who was in the position of governor. Therefore, he changed the direction of a stream to Sangchon village in order to suppress the auspiciousness of Mokchon. This was done because the landscape of the Kim village was the type of a silkworm's head, and therefore the silkworm could not cross the stream to reach the mulberry grove. In addition, he removed the mulberry trees and planted lacquer trees in order to kill the silkworm. After that, the Kim family lost its fortune and declined.[14]

This allegorical understanding of landscape was also an aesthetic evaluation. Geomancers saw "beauty" as a clear indication of auspiciousness, and often modifications were made to the landscape principally to improve its appearance and thus one's fortune. Indeed, Needham credits geomancy with responsibility for the "exceptional beauty of the positioning of farmhouses, manors, villages and cities throughout the realm of the Chinese culture."[15]

Because the garden was built within the context of a greater landscape, its siting had to be integrated with the macropatterns of the

region. And because it used the real substances of earth—stones, trees, and water—the micropatterns of ch'i had to be coordinated within the garden. The garden artist had to discern the veins of energy contained within the stones and harmonize the currents between them. Paths, river courses, and other shapes generated their own currents which also had to be fully harmonized with each other.

Thus seen through the eyes of a geomancer, the artificially constructed environment which we today call a garden had many different levels of meaning. It was made to be the most ideal of landscapes, designed to bring the best possible luck. It was both beautiful, for beauty is a sign of good fortune, and functional, as it manipulated the local currents of ch'i for maximum benefit. The beautiful landscape was the geomantically correct landscape.

City and Garden Design

Kyoto is a clear example of a site designed according to geomantic principles (Fig. 13.11). It lies on a flat plane protected by mountains on all sides except the south, which is the auspicious direction. In the northeast corner, or "Demon Gate," stands the highest mountain

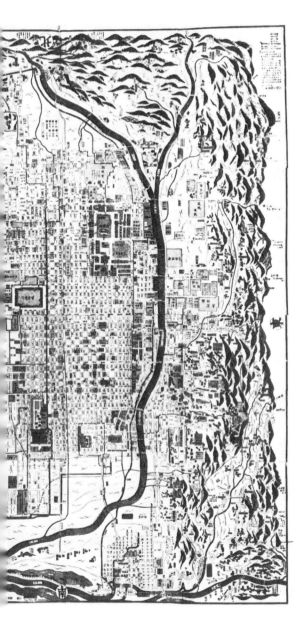

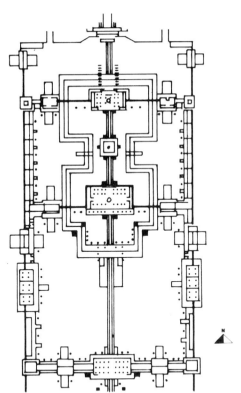

fig. 13.10 (opposite, above) *An early thirteenth-century map showing an auspicious topographic site for a Chinese temple. Note that the configuration of the rivers and mountains is similar to that of Kyoto (fig. 13.11). (From Ti Li Cho Yu Fu, twelfth century, after Needham, vol. 4, part 1.)*

fig. 13.11 (above) *Map of Kyoto showing its geomantically favorable site. (Collection of Ozuka Takushi.)*

fig. 13.12 (above, right) *Plan of the Forbidden City in Peking clearly illustrates the strong axial symmetry, the hierarchical progression of buildings, and the stress on ceremonial sequence of spaces. Buddhist temple compounds were generally, but not rigidly, based on these same planning principles.*

in the area, Mt. Hiei, which acts as a guardian. The Kamogawa River flows in the appropriate direction (northeast to southwest) and bends slightly around the city so that Kyoto lies "within the belly of the dragon," protected from the forces of evil and in an area of concentrated *ch'i*. Although this river originally ran diagonally through the city site, its course was altered to the present one in order to bring it into compliance with geomantic and town planning practices. We see numerous similar orientations in Kyoto gardens (Fig. 14.6).

The plan of Kyoto was based on the Chinese T'ang dynasty capital of Ch'ang-an. The overall grid plan was bisected by a long north–south avenue that led to the Emperor's palace. Inside the palace, the avenue continued, passing the symmetrically arranged buildings of state in order of increasing importance, until the Imperial way reached the Emperor's throne (Fig. 13.12). The same principles of city and palace layout were also adopted for Buddhist temples, where icons were substituted for the throne at the end of the main axis. This plan, whether for cities or temples, was believed to replicate aspects of the universal design. In these compounds, priests and emperors performed the rites that ensured continued existence.

The first gardens may have also played some ceremonial role, but our only picture of them comes from literary accounts. Time and continuous internal turmoil have taken a heavy toll on the architecture and gardens of China. The surviving Chinese gardens and paintings of gardens date from relatively late eras. But the Chinese tradition is a slow and conservative one, and we can imagine that the remaining fragments, along with literary descriptions, offer us some glimpses of earlier gardens. What readily appears is that Japanese gardens developed into something very different from Chinese gardens. A few comparisons will suffice: The preferred Chinese garden stone was full of holes and hollows eroded by water, indicating the fluid nature of the universe. The Japanese never seem to have adopted stones like these, preferring instead quieter stones with level heads or a resemblance to mountains. The severe geometry of Chinese paths and bridges with zigzags and high arches were usually toned down by the Japanese into smoother shapes. Door openings through garden walls were often elaborate in the Chinese versions, but are usually quite simple in Japanese gardens (Figs. 13.13 and 13.14). This can be said for the whole of Japanese garden architecture and its details. While the Japanese inherited the ideas of garden making from the Chinese, they soon adapted form and details to suit their own climate, temperament, and budgets.

We can, however, trace some elements of Japanese garden forms back to early Chinese gardens. The crane and turtle shapes come from an old Chinese myth regarding the islands of the immortals: Far off in the western seas lie islands supported on the backs of giant turtles (Figs. 2.12 and 6.13). Here the immortals dwell in eternal bliss accompanied by large cranes who carry them about. Appropriately shaped garden islands and stone groupings, usually found in a set (the turtle is yang, the crane yin), are particularly auspicious garden forms that have come to mean long life. One story tells that the Emperor Wu of the former Han Dynasty (260 B.C.–A.D. 9) even went so far as to construct large artificial islands in the hopes of luring some immortals to his garden.[16]

Another important feature of early Japanese gardens was the centrally located large stone hill used to represent Shumisen, pivotal mountain of the Buddhist cosmos. An analysis of Shumisen sheds some light on medieval Chinese and Japanese conceptions of geography and cosmology. About the time the

Japanese first started building gardens, in the seventh century, a Chinese Buddhist pilgrim who had traveled through India and Southeast Asia in his search for the true law thus described the makeup of the universe:

The mountain called *Sumeru* [Shumisen] stands in the midst of the great sea firmly fixed on a

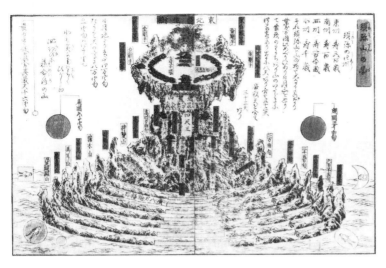

fig. 13.13 (opposite, above) *Traditional rockwork, wall and door opening in a Ming dynasty (1368–1644) garden. Private home and garden, Hongchow. (From* **Chinese Homes and Gardens** *by Henry Inn, copyright, permission by Hastings House Publisher, New York, 1950.)*

fig. 13.14 (opposite, below) *Although it was built at approximately the same time as the Chinese garden of fig. 13.13, the garden of Kohoan (1644) reveals an entirely different kind of design spirit.*

fig. 13.15 (left) *An Edo period representation of hour-glass-shaped Shumisen surrounded by the concentric rings of seas and mountains. The inhabited islands are represented by the people inscribed inside the shapes situated in the outermost sea. (Collection of Mitchell Bring.)*

circle of gold, around which the sun and the moon revolve; this mountain is composed of four precious substances, and is the abode of the gods. Around this there are seven mountain ranges and seven seas; outside the seven golden mountain ranges is the salt sea. There are four islands in this salt sea, which are inhabited by humans.[17]

The southernmost island in the salt sea contained the known world, which was divided into quadrants: China in the east, which was ruled by the "lord of men"; India in the south, "where the people are given to learning . . . especially the magical arts" Mongolia and Siberia in the north, where people "are naturally wild and fierce" and ruled by the "lord of horses"; and Arabia in the west, the "land of gems where people have no politeness or justice and they accumulate wealth."[18]

The presence of Shumisen in early Japanese gardens indicates that Japan too used Buddhist cosmologic models. The notion of a great central mountain seems to be found throughout Asia, perhaps having its origins in Mesopotamia.[19] Shumisen, with its many concentric rings of mountains, is pictured as an hourglass (Fig. 13.15) and has been called the "Nine Mountains and Eight Seas." A stone with carved ridges of similar design pattern was unearthed at the site of an Asuka period (552–710) garden,[20] while there is a stone bearing this name in the garden of Kinkakuji (Fig. 3.15). Although it is centrally located, the small size of Kinkakuji's stone seems to indicate that by the fourteenth century the Japanese no longer took the concept literally. In early gardens built to mirror the workings of the heavens, however, the model of Shumisen may have been the prominent central feature.

NOTES

[1]Philip Rawson and Laszlo Legeza, *Tao: The Chinese Philosophy of Time and Change,* Thames and Hudson, London, 1973, p. 13.

[2]Andrew Boyd, *Chinese Architecture 1500 B.C.–A.D. 1911,* Alec Tiranti, London, 1962, pp. 111–112.

[3]H. Chatley, "Feng-shui," *Encyclopedia Sinica,* Kelly and Walsh, Shanghai, 1917.

[4]E. J. Eitel, *Feng-shui; Principles of the Natural Science of the Chinese,* Lane, Crawford, Hong Kong, 1873.

[5]Joseph Needham, *Science and Civilization in China,* vol. 2, Cambridge University Press, 1959, p. 359.

[6]Loraine Kuck, *The World of the Japanese Garden,* Walker/Weatherhill, Tokyo, 1968, p. 241.

[7]Josiah Conder, *Landscape Gardening of Japan,* 1893, Dover reprint, New York, 1963.

[8]Paul Wheatley, *The Pivot of the Four Corners,* Edinburgh University Press, 1971, p. 419.

[9]Cheng Ssu-Hsiao, *So-Nan Wen Chi* (Collected Writings of Cheng Ssu-Hsiao, 1340), translated by Joseph Needham, *Science and Civilization in China,* vol. 3, Cambridge University Press, 1959, p. 650.

[10]Ibid.

[11]Choi Sangsu, *Hankuk Mingan Chonsoljip,* translated by Hong-Key Yoon, *Geomantic Relationships between Culture and Nature in Korea,* Orient Cultural Service, Taipei, 1976, p. 214.

[12]For a complete description of how the compass is used, see Stephan D. R. Feuchtwang, *An Anthropological Analysis of Chinese Geomancy,* Editions Vithogna, Vientiane, Laos, 1974.

[13]Meng T'ien (d. 210), *Shih Chi,* translated by Joseph Needham, *Science and Civilization in China,* vol. 4, part 1, Cambridge University Press, 1962, p. 240.

[14]Hong-Key Yoon, *Geomantic Relationships between Culture and Nature in Korea,* Orient Cultural Service, Taipei, 1976, p. 142.

[15]Needham, op. cit., vol. 2, p. 361.

[16]Kuck, op. cit., p. 43.

[17]Samuel Beal, translator, *Buddhist Records of the Western World,* Trüber, London, 1906, pp. 10–17.

[18]Ibid.

[19]H. G. Quaritch Wales, "The Sacred Mountain in Old Asiatic Religion," *Journal of the Royal Asiatic Society,* London, 1953, p. 23.

[20]See Teiichi Shigeta, "Asuka no Shumisen" ("An Asuka-Period Shumisen"), *Shigaku Zasshi (History Magazine),* vol. 15, January 1904, pp. 47–54. See also *Asuka Shiryokan: Annai,* (Guide to the Asuka Historical Museum), Nara National Cultural Properties Research Institute, Nara 1975.

chapter fourteen

Japanese Synthesis

After the death of the historical Buddha in the fifth century B.C., Buddhist teachings spread eastward from India, reaching China in the first century A.D., Korea in the fourth century, and Japan in the sixth century. During this journey of a thousand years, across thousands of miles, the original teachings of the Enlightened One were transformed not only by contact with the indigenous cultures of the lands that they passed through but also by subsequent developments in religious thinking. These forces gave rise to a number of different sects and cults that spanned a broad philosophical spectrum. Two of these sects, Pure Land Buddhism and Zen Buddhism, provided strong impetus for garden making, but they did so for entirely different reasons.

THE IMAGE OF PARADISE

An Indian text that reached China in the fifth century portrayed the Pure Land or Western Paradise of Amida Buddha as a magnificent courtyard of sensual pleasures, including a pond of the purest water, the most fragrant and beautiful bejeweled plants, the rarest and most wonderful birds performing celestial concerts.[1] By the seventh century, this paradise came to be pictured graphically in terms of its best-known earthly counterpart, the Chinese imperial park (Fig. 14.1). Adopting the same imagery, the eleventh-century Heian aristocracy built mansions that attempted to recreate the Western Paradise on earth.[2]

The Byodo-in's Phoenix Hall is the last remaining portion of one such attempt (Fig. 14.2). Its Chinese T'ang style central hall houses an image of the Amida Buddha and sits on the west bank of a lotus pond. The orientation differs from the usual north–south temple configuration, allowing the Amida image to be positioned on the west side of the garden in the direction of paradise. The original Phoenix Hall garden no longer exists, but a contemporary description of another garden of the same period reveals much about the style of the later Heian age:

He who gave his attention in tranquillity to the appearance of the precinct's interior, [would have seen] the sand of the courtyard sparkling like crystal. The water of the pond pure and clear, with all manner of lotus flowers growing in it . . . . surrounding the pond trees were planted, from all the branches of which were suspended silk nets. A bridge made of the Seven Precious Things spanned this gold and jade pool; vessels made of diverse precious

fig. 14.1 (upper) *The Shokai Mandala is a graphic representation of the Buddhist Pure Land. This 1726 copy is believed to be a faithful reproduction of the 996 original (owned by Shokoji Temple, Kyoto.)*

fig. 14.2 (lower) *The Phoenix Hall of the Byodo-in in Uji, south of Kyoto. This structure, built in 1052, takes its form and many details from Chinese T'ang Dynasty (618–907) palaces that were shown in paintings of the Buddhist Pure Land.*

things went to and fro among the reflections of the trees; while peacocks and parrots played on the central island. . . . The roof tiles of pearl of the "jewelled towers" lent the green of their covering; glazed walls, the whiteness, of their coat. The gleam of the tiles reflected the sky; there were column bases of ivory, ridges of red gold, gilded doors, platforms of crystal. Thus were they adorned and made majestic with every sort of varied treasure. . . .[3]

These *shinden* style mansion-temples, of which the Byodo-in was a part, have been called "one of the happiest products of Heian cultural fusion . . . combining the pomp of the Chinese palace, the intimacy of the Japanese home, and the otherworldliness of the Buddhist temple."[4] As settings for everyday living, they must have indeed seemed like paradise to the Heian courtiers.

The *shinden* compound was divided into two parts, consisting of main buildings in the north and the garden in the south (Fig. 14.3). The central structure was the *shinden*, the oblong main hall, flanked on either side by buildings that served as the family quarters. Perpendicular to these buildings were covered corridors that projected out into the garden itself, each ending in some sort of pavilion that sat on piles above the pond and bore a name such as the fishing pavilion or the spring pavilion. The enduring popularity of this feature has been mentioned in the introduction and in the separate garden chapters.

Originally the *shinden* compound adhered to Chinese dictates of strict symmetry, but in the later estates the design became more irregular and informal, reflecting native Japanese preferences. On the whole, only the richest noble could afford to execute the entire plan, and considerable variation on the theme took place.

fig. 14.3 *Hypothetical reconstruction of a* shinden *style compound, from a wood-block illustration found in the mid-nineteenth-century book* Kaoku Zakko. *Note the covered walkways linking the buildings and the pondside pavilions.*

The garden contained the traditional features of the Chinese garden: a pond with islands reached by bridges; artificial knolls, some with a central mountain or stone composition representing Shumisen; and a small stream flowing down from the north. The front central area was covered with white sand and served as grounds for ceremonies and entertainments.

Tachibana Toshitsuna (1028–1094), son of the regent Fujiwara Yorimichi who built the Byodo-in, codified the rules for making *shinden* gardens. Entitled the *Sakuteiki*, his work was expanded in 1289 and has been handed down through the ages as a treasured book of secrets. It is perhaps the world's oldest gardening manual, offering instructions on geomantic, aesthetic, and practical matters. Although the *shinden* style mansion did not survive into the Medieval Age, the principles of design outlined in the *Sakuteiki*, as well as Pure Land imagery, endured in modified forms as has been noted for Saihoji, Kinkakuji, Ginkakuji, and Sambo-in.

Sakuteiki: The Book of Garden[5]

Geomancy Heian society had incorporated Chinese teachings of astronomy, astrology, and geomancy to such a degree that a sizable portion of the literature describes the court members' preoccupation with auspicious days and directions.[6] Harmonizing with the great forces was so important that a government ministry of yin and yang affairs was established to advise the court on these matters. Geomantic taboos listed in the *Sakuteiki* are a mixture of the adopted Chinese system and native elements. For the Japanese, the new practice of moving stones for garden purposes—without arousing the wrath of the spirits Shinto knew to be inside—required careful attention to the geomantic rules outlined by Chinese science. The *Sakuteiki* illustrates this tradition of conservatism by warning a would-be garden maker that "even these matters [geomantic taboos] you should be mindful of" and citing "a certain Chinese person of the Sung dynasty" as a respectable authority.

The great majority of taboos listed in the *Sakuteiki* involve the proper and improper use of stones, followed by concerns about waterfalls, the correct selection and placement of trees, and the proper courses of stream flows. The taboos indicate the bad fortune that results from ignoring correct relationships with the cosmic forces:

There are many taboos concerning the placing of stones. It is said that if even one of them is violated, the master of the house would constantly suffer from illness to the ultimate loss of his life, and that the place would be deserted to become an abode of demons. . . .

[For example] Do not place stones close to the southwest pillar of the house. It is said that if you violate this the household would be constantly harassed by illnesses. . . .

In making a garden by modelling after a certain famous landscape, do not try to simulate such a place if the land which was once famous has become desolate. This is because the reproducing of a dilapidated scene in front of one's house should be avoided. . .

When you make the scene of a hill, do not let the valley point toward the house. If you do so, they say, ill luck will befall the women facing it and so on. In general, the opening of the valley should not face the main front view of the garden, but instead a little away from it. . . .

Placing sideways the stone which was originally set vertically, or setting the stone upright which was originally laid sideways, is taboo. If this taboo is violated, the stone will surely become the "stone of revengeful spirits" and will bring a curse.

Heian Japanese were tremendously literal and believed the written Chinese character had magical qualities in itself. For example, the character for water is still placed on wooden buildings to protect them from fire. Consequently, the shape of garden forms was very important:

Water always assumes its shape depending on the container (and the shape of the pond itself affects the good or evil omen). The pond may also be dug in the form of some auspicious word written in the cursive style. [A clear example can be seen in the Saihoji pond, which is in the shape of the character for heart.]

. . . If there is a tree in the center of an enclosed ground, the master of the house would always be in trouble. The reason for this is that the tree in the center of an enclosure forms the Chinese character which means "distress" [Fig. 14.4, left].

fig. 14.4 Left side: *The Chinese character* **komaru**, *meaning trouble, is symbolized by a single enclosed tree.* **Right side:** *The Chinese character* p'in (shina *in Japanese*). *Tachibana Toshitsuna, the author of the* **Sakuteiki**, *intends the character to be used as a plan for positioning stones, one in back and two in front.*

In accordance with the flow of *ch'i*, the direction of the stream course is also very important:

For this reason, the garden stream of the main courtyard also should come out from the east side of the main hall or other main structures and flow first toward the west. Even when the stream starts at the north side, it should be led first toward the east, and then toward the south west.

The book further says that the inner side of the stream curve represents the belly of the dragon (Fig. 13.10) and that the dwelling house built on that side foretells good luck, while placing the house on the outer side of the curve, or the back of the dragon, brings ill luck to the dweller.

There is another doctrine of directing the water coming from the north straight to the south. This probably means that north denotes the element of water, and the south, fire. The harmony will be effected by the meeting of Yin and Yang, or the positive and negative. Thus the practice is not without its reason.

The practice of balancing the site also carried into tree planting:

Concerning the planting of trees in the four cardinal directions around the dwelling of man, and [satisfying] the doctrine of the four Gods [gods of the directions]. . . . [Thus] If there is no flowing water on the east side of the house, plant 9 willow trees there. . . . If there is no big road on the west, plant 7 catalpa trees there. . . . If there is no pond on the south, plant 9 cinnamon trees. . . . If there are no hills to the north, plant 3 Japanese cypress trees.

It is said that once one makes one's land conform to the doctrine of the four Gods and dwells therein, one would be endowed with his official rank, fortune and stipend, as well as his good health and long life [Fig. 14.5].

In the *Sakuteiki*, therefore, the garden is seen to be more than an attractive surrounding: It functions almost as a magical talisman to ensure both good health and prosperity. It is an optimum landscape designed to provide the best of all possible worlds, harmonizing with the great earth forces as well as with the eye. Figures 14.6 and 14.7 indicate remnants of these practices found in the surveyed gardens.

Practical instructions The *Sakuteiki* also contains some practical advice concerning the construction of the garden. It emphasizes that each garden is a separate work of design, with site topology the primary consideration:

In designing landscape works, first the topology of the site should be studied; next ponds shaped, then islands arranged by results of the survey; finally pond water supply and flowout [points] should be decided . . . . to plan island landscapes, it depends on garden site conditions and the space of the ponds. After the islands are planned next they are roughly cut and rocks are positioned before detailed shaping. The buildings near the ponds are constructed before [ponds] are actually filled with water, care being taken with water level instruments to position the underside of the kiosk verandah 6 inches above the projected water level [Fig. 1.7].

The *Sakuteiki* takes great care with the details of the waterworks:

After setting the elevations for the course of the running stream, if you make the ratio of the drop of the elevation to the distance of the running stream to be three to one hundred [3%], the stream will flow smoothly with a murmuring sound. If it is difficult to dig the channel and flush it with water at the time of construction, in order to set the elevations, lay pieces of split bamboo on the ground with the hollow sides up, run water through them and determine the elevations. To build the house and garden without first making these preparations shows ignorance of the matter . . . . the placing of stones for the garden stream should start at a place where it makes a turn and flows along. This turn is supposed to have been caused by the presence of the rock which the stream could not demolish.

fig. 14.5 *A modern-day attempt at using garden trees to satisfy the dictates of direction. On this portion of the geomancer's chart, each plant is shown in conjunction with one of the twelve cardinal directions and one of the symbolic animals (see fig. 13.8). This chart is displayed at various monthly festivals held in Kyoto at Toji Temple and Kitano Shrine.*

fig. 14.6 *Table showing the various garden orientations and geomantic relationships.*

Garden	Building Orientation	Stream Course
Saihoji	Magnetic north, i.e., 5 to 10° west of true north	Stream enters from the west. This is the only instance of such a course and may be due in part to the garden's original allusion to the Western paradise.
Kinkakuji	Antimagnetic north, i.e., 5 to 10° east of true north	Waterfall is north of the building. Another stream enters the pond in the northeast corner, and the stream exits in the southwest. This is the traditional course described in the *Sakuteiki*.
Ginkakuji	Antimagnetic north, front of Silver Pavilion faces east.	Spring located in northeast corner, feeding a stream that flows first west then south. Waterfall is east of the pavilion. The stream exits in the southwest (see Fig. 14-7).
Ryoanji	Magnetic north	The stones of the symbolic composition appear to be flowing east to west.
Daisen-in	Magnetic north	The symbolic waterfall in the northeast corner feeds two sand "streams," one flowing south and the other west.
Sambo-in	Antimagnetic north	Two waterfalls in the northeast and southeast corners feed the pond. Water flows out of the pond on the west side.
Shodenji	Antimagnetic north Building faces east	Shrubs increase in size from north to south.
Entsuji	Antimagnetic north Building faces east	The greatest concentration of stones is in the northeast corner. The stones represent a river flowing southward.
Shisendo	Antimagnetic north	There is a waterfall in the northeast corner that feeds a stream flowing first to the west and then to the south. Water leaves the site in the southwest.
Kohoan	True north	Orientation uncertain for the symbolic river.

There are also some practical points about living with the garden. "Do not place a stone where rainwater (from the house eaves) drops upon it. A person getting the spray of such raindrops would contact bad skin diseases because of the poisonous effect of water which comes down from the cypress-bark roofing and hits that stone. Someone says that many woodsmen working in cypress forests suffer from certain skin troubles on their feet."

Apparently this has some basis in fact. Referring to the water contained in the artificial basin formed around a spring, the *Sakuteiki* advises ". . . the water will smell bad after one or two nights and insects will come out of it, therefore the fountain must flow regularly and the bottom stones [should be] washed."

Aesthetics The aesthetics of the *Sakuteiki* are best illustrated in its own opening words:

In making the garden, you should first understand the overall principles.
1. According to the lay of the land, and depending upon the aspect of the water landscape, you should design each part of the garden tastefully, recalling your memories of how nature presented itself for each feature.
2. Study the examples of works left by the past masters, and, considering the desires of the owner of the garden, you should create a work of your own by exercising your tasteful sense.
3. Think over the famous places of scenic beauty throughout the land, and by making it your own that which appeals to you most, design your garden with the mood of harmony, modelling after the general air of such places.

Comparing the randomness of beauty found in nature to that of the studied perfection of art, the *Sakuteiki* explains:

Some person has remarked that the stones placed and the sceneries made by man can never excel the landscape in nature. Nevertheless, visiting through many provinces I have noted [on] several occasions that when I was deeply impressed by the excellence of a

N = North
MN = Magnetic North
AMN = Antimagnetic north
E = East

certain scenic beauty, I also found some worthless views close by renowned scenery. In the case of a man-made landscape garden, since only the attractive and best parts of the places are studied and modelled after, meaningless stones and features are seldom provided along with man's work.

In making the garden, first the pond shape and then the rock work determined the artistic theme, with plant material used to reinforce the effect. Thus, the *Sakuteiki* distinguishes five distinct styles of rock landscape, adding that these styles can be mixed as space permits. The five styles are ocean, river, valley, marsh, and waving reed style; each is determined by the sculptural and textural qualities of the stones utilized in achieving the desired scenery. Two of the styles are contrasted:

In this style [ocean], first construct the scene of a rough seashore, placing there some pointed rocks in a casual looking manner. Then place a sequence of rocks from the shore toward the offing, making them appear as though the rocks had grown out of the same bedrock extending from the shore. There should be a few rocks isolated from the rest. As these rocks are ruthlessly exposed to the billows, they should look like they had been washed out. Finally you should provide here and there views of the sandbank and white beach where some black pines may be planted. . . .

The hills and mounds in this style of landscape [waving reed] should not be prominent. The stones [are] placed here and there toward the end of the hillside field or at the pond shore, and are associated with low plants such as the grass bamboo, mountain sedge and the like. As for the trees to be planted, preferences should be given to those of soft forms like the plum tree and the weeping willow. As a rule, flat stones are used for this style of landscape, often laying them in the form of the Chinese character *P'in* (Japanese, *shina*). . . .[Fig. 14.4, right].

Islands are similarly categorized according to feeling, specific type, or shape: field island, forest island, rocky-shore island, cloud shape, mist shape, sandy-beach type, running-stream style, ebb-tide style, and pine-bark pattern.

Waterfalls, which are given a great deal of attention, are categorized according to texture and form: running fall, cloth fall, double-stepping fall, and so forth. The width of waterfalls seems to be related to their height:

When we observe natural waterfalls we notice that tall falls are not necessarily wide, nor low falls always narrow in breadth. They only depend on the breadth of the lip of the stone over which the water falls. However, for a waterfall three or four feet high, its breadth should not exceed two feet. The low waterfall with a broad width has several disadvantages. In the first place, the waterfall itself looks low. Second, it is mistaken for a river dam. Another point is that the crest of the falls is often exposed to full view, making the scene lacking in depth. The waterfall presents a darkened and deep atmosphere when it is seen falling from an unexpected ravine surrounded by rocks. For this reason it is advisable to put a good looking stone where the outlet of the falling water is exposed to view. This makes the waterfall appear, when seen from a distance, as though it were falling out of the mountain rocks.

Stones can be used not only in the direct recreation of scenery but also symbolically or sculpturally: "The stones placed at the foot of the hill or in the hillside plain should resemble a pack of dogs crouching on the ground, or running and scattering a group of pigs, or else a calf playing near the sitting mother cow." Another common composition suggested the *Sanzon* triad of Buddha with two attendants, usually represented by the largest triangular grouping. Here is an allegorical projection of meaning similar to interpretations by the Chinese geomancer of full-scale landscapes. In a garden, the diverse meanings seen in stones account for their primary importance in construction.

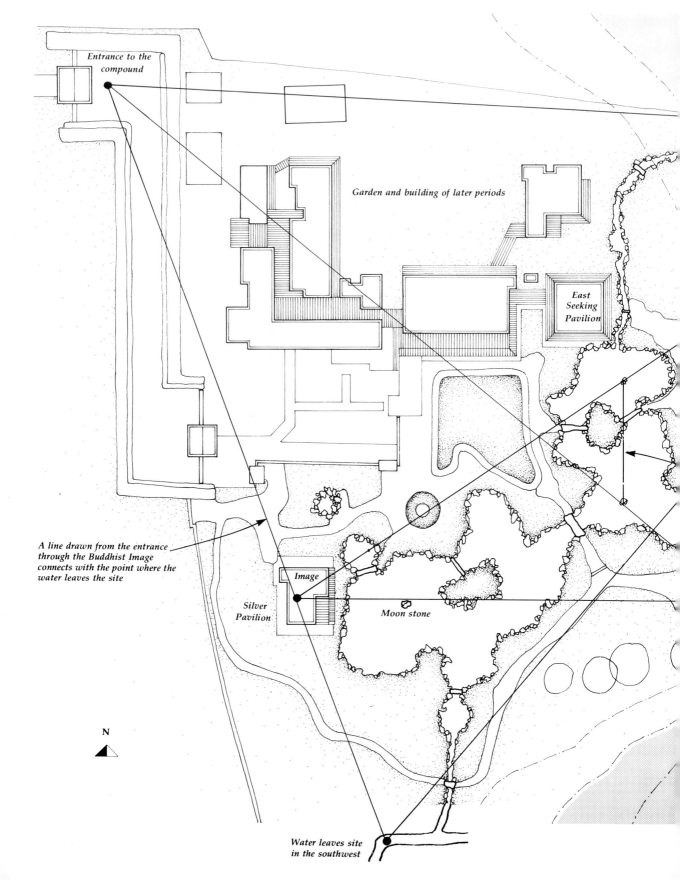

Entrance to the
compound

Garden and building of later periods

East
Seeking
Pavilion

A line drawn from the entrance
through the Buddhist Image
connects with the point where the
water leaves the site

Image

Silver
Pavilion

Moon stone

N

Water leaves site
in the southwest

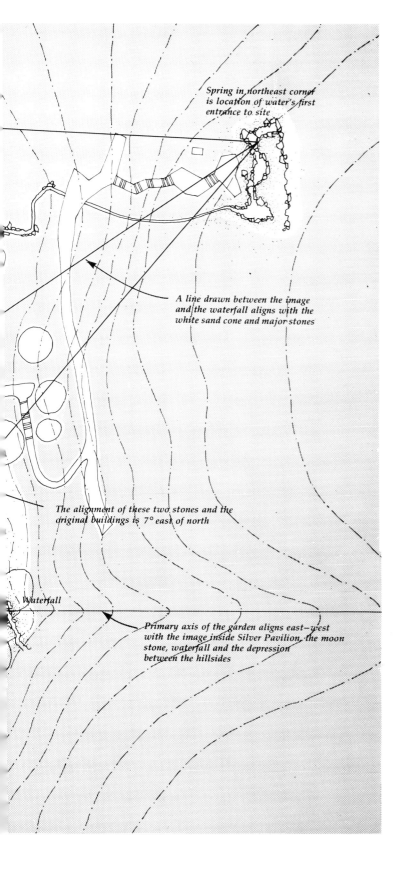

Spring in northeast corner
is location of water's first
entrance to site

A line drawn between the image
and the waterfall aligns with the
white sand cone and major stones

The alignment of these two stones and the
original buildings is 7° east of north

Waterfall

Primary axis of the garden aligns east–west
with the image inside Silver Pavilion, the moon
stone, waterfall and the depression
between the hillsides

fig. 14.7 *Hypothetical
reconstruction of geomantic
design factors in the plan of
Ginkakuji.* **Note:** *This is based
on fig. 4.5.*

ZEN LANDSCAPES

The emergence of Zen as a design force can be illustrated by the story of Saihoji's name. The original reading of Saihoji meant "Temple of the Western Direction," which, of course, refers to the Pure Land of the Western Paradise. When the temple became a Zen temple in the fourteenth century, the Zen monks, with characteristic subtlety, changed the Chinese characters to mean "Temple of the Western Fragrance," a Zen allusion, though the pronunciation remained the same. In a similar spirit, when the bright flowering trees of Saihoji died, they were not replaced, so that the garden now has a mood more characteristic of a Zen garden.

Known as Ch'an in China, the Zen sect reached a level of prominence there in the ninth century but did not become finally established in Japan until the thirteenth century. Zen was the last great school of Buddhism, distinguished—by its philosophical distrust of intellectual dogma and value of life's mundane aspects—from the highly esoteric and otherworldly teachings of later Buddhist sects. Consequently, Zen art turned away from the supernatural, the symmetrical, and colorful ostentation, emphasizing instead natural, asymmetric, and monochromatic compositions. For garden making, it helped bring the ideal image out of the heavens and down to earth. Zen canons of taste had an all-pervasive effect on Japanese culture, so that it is almost impossible to speak of Japanese art without speaking of Zen.

The reasons for the Zen sect's rise to power, and the consequent role it would play in the arts, had much to do with the political situation at the time of its introduction. The Medieval Age began when power was transferred from the Heian court to a military government in Kamakura near Tokyo. The move was partially prompted by the desire of the new leaders to avoid the intrigues of court politics and the established power of older Buddhist sects in Kyoto. The relatively new sect of Zen offered a nontextual doctrine, one that stressed self-reliance and discipline, aspects which greatly appealed to the military consciousness. When Japan was threatened in the thirteenth century by the Mongols of Genghis Khan who had conquered China and Korea, the military leaders turned to the Zen monks, many of whom were Chinese refugees, fiercely anti-Mongol and familiar with the latest teachings

and knowledge of their continent. Thus serving the government, the Zen monks became trusted advisers on all matters from "taxes to tea cult." From the fourteenth century they served as principal agents of trade with China, even acting as art merchants to finance new temple construction, and as suppliers and connoisseurs they became the undisputed arbiters of taste, self-consciously reshaping Japanese culture in the process.

The key distinction of Zen philosophy is that it viewed enlightenment not as something that came from without—through mastery of a magic formula or the help of a supernatural being—but as a direct, self-sought experience of the "here and now" brought about through meditation and the guidance of a master. Thus, Zen art largely dispensed with the elaborate Buddhist pantheon and concentrated on trying to capture the essence or spirit of things, preferring to paint monochrome landscapes rather than brilliant pictures of paradise. The mountains and rivers of the earth were then seen in Chinese terms of natural beauty and harmony, not as lowly manifestations that needed to be forsaken for the glory of paradise.

The practice of meditating for long hours, sitting completely erect, with the mind a calm pool of water mirroring the world around it, went hand in hand with the practice of Zen arts. One could not paint the essence of things without seeing them, nor could one arrange garden stones without feeling their spirit. For

fig. 14.8 *Mountain landscape, detail from a painting in the set entitled* **Eight Views of the Hsiao,** *by Yu Chien (c. 1350). (Collection of Ayako Yoshikawa, Tokyo.)*

the Zen monk, one's art is thus a measure of one's spiritual insight.

In painting, Japanese art became more and more abstract as the monk painters sought to bring out only the essential qualities of their subjects. A single brushstroke could represent a massive mountain or the beak of a sparrow. Dynamic tension and balance became important features of painting, and the result is a visual art that looks strikingly "modern" to our eyes (Fig. 14.8).

In landscape gardening there was a similar tendency to move toward simpler but more expressive design. This search for the essential reached the conclusion found in Ryoanji (Fig. 5.5), where trees, bushes, and water have been omitted entirely, leaving only fifteen stones, sand, and moss to suggest a great landscape. The practice of *karesansui* (dry gardening) was utilized in Zen gardens partially out of necessity and partially in service to the creation of an image reminiscent of the Sung Dynasty Chinese landscape paintings. These scenes, which usually pictured the dramatic angular mountains and great river valleys of China, were the prototypes for both Japanese landscape painting and garden making. Thus the miniature landscapes found in Zen gardens were often based on Chinese, not Japanese, countryside. Frequently the same monk was both painter and garden maker, like Soami of Daisen-in, and obviously the two art forms shared much in terms of style and technique (Fig. 6.12). In Daisen-in, stones and plants may have been selected because they looked like the brushstroke renderings of the masters—a classic example of life imitating art. Chapter 15 discusses some further similarities in the design principles used in landscape painting and gardening.

In gardens that were not originally built for monasteries, such as Saihoji and Ginkakuji, the relationship to Zen landscape art is less obvious but still apparent. In Ginkakuji, for example, there are many surviving vestiges of the Pure Land tradition such as the pond and the east–west orientation of the pavilion (which contains a Pure Land image), but the stone composition of the islands and bridges seems directly derived from the Zen painting gardening tradition. The later gardens of Entsuji and Shodenji illustrate a modified form of Zen gardening that used less stark materials to generate less realistic renditions of miniature landscapes.

TEA GARDENS

The practice of drinking tea to fend off drowsiness during meditation was introduced to Japan by the Zen monks, who imported the beverage from China. Powdered tea was whisked with boiling water to form a frothy brew that was passed from one monk to another during a communal ceremony before meditation. The monks in turn introduced tea to members of the military aristocracy, who held parties during which guests competed with each other in identifying the origin and nature of the tea.

Muso Kokushi (1275–1351) was one of the few monks who possessed Chinese equipment for making and serving tea, and he must have entertained guests in the garden pavilions of Saihoji. But the basic way of serving tea known today developed during the reign of Ashikaga Yoshimasa under the tutelage of his tea master and garden designer, Shuko (1422–1503). Here, drinking tea became a fine aesthetic ritual during which a gathering of associates, guided by their host or tea master, partook of the painstakingly prepared drink. A building in Yoshimasa's Ginkakuji garden, the Togudo (East Seeking Pavilion), was specially adapted for this purpose and embodies many prototypical tea room features: the four-and-one-half tatami-mat format, a central firebox for the kettle, and an open alcove with ornamental shelves (tokonoma) that found its way out of the tea room to become a standard feature of the Japanese home. The room design, the few works of art displayed in it, and the utensils for making tea were all selected with a fine eye for detail and harmony. Although the ritual was held in a garden setting, the gardens of this time were not explicitly designed for the way of tea. It was not until the time of the great tea master Sen no Rikkyu (1521–1591), a contemporary and associate of Hideyoshi's, that a distinct tea garden form—the *roji* (cottage path or cleared ground)—was developed. These early garden models as well as other features of the ceremony were refined and elaborated on by such people as Kobori Enshu (1579–1647), whose garden at Kohoan embodies a mature and distinctive style.[7]

The spirit of these gardens came in part from the image of the retreat of the Chinese hermit scholar (Fig. 13.4). The resurgence of Chinese scholarship outside the monasteries, beginning around the turn of the seventeenth century, went hand in hand with the development of the way of tea. Many upper-class Japanese wanted nothing more than a tranquil life given over to the study of Chinese classics surrounded by nature, as this letter by Ishikawa Jozan (1583–1672), the maker of Shisendo, reveals:

Sometimes I pick flowers in the garden and make them the companions of my heart. Or I listen to the first wild geese and treat them as my guests. Sometimes I open my brushwood gate and sweep out the leaves, or I look into the old garden and plant chrysanthemums. Sometimes I climb the eastern hill and sing to the moon, or I draw my chair to the northern window and read books and recite poetry. Apart from these pursuits I do nothing.[8]

Quiet solitude amid nature, so often depicted in literature and painting, is termed *wabi* by the Japanese. The tea garden is principally designed to convey this rustic tranquillity and is called *roji* after its principal feature, the "cottage" pathway. The path represents a psychological transition to the tea room's rarefied atmosphere. One is journeying to the home of a hermit and must enter his frame of mind, putting aside all worldly cares.

The spatial sequence of the garden is carefully orchestrated by a series of fences and gateways symbolizing the various internal changes taking place. Along the path, people stop to wash their hands, an echo of the Shinto act of purification, and then enter the tea house through a small door. Bending down to enter through this door is an act of physical humility, and visitors cross the threshold as different people. Once inside, they cannot see the garden: It is blocked from view by opaque paper window shades that are kept closed during the ceremony (Fig. 14.9). The pathway is like the set for a psychodrama in which the participants act out a transformation of character in their return to nature for spiritual rejuvenation.

Perhaps the most obvious departure from earlier gardens is that the stones are relatively few and unobtrusive. The preferred plants are common evergreen varieties that grow naturally along paths in the countryside. Ornamental and flowering trees—except for the plum tree with its white blossoms in late February—are avoided because they would disturb the overall tranquillity and "naturalness" of the scene. The way of tea prefers natural finishes, such as thatched roofs and unhewn wood for the tea room, and earthenware tea bowls.[9] The garden materials are selected with an eye for a naturally aged and weathered look that is termed *sabi*. This patina of age makes the garden seem ancient and is meant to inspire feelings of profundity and deep contemplation. Though aged-looking, the garden setting is immaculately kept,

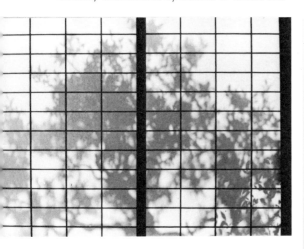

fig. 14.9 (above) *Shadows cast by the garden plants create patterns on the* shoji *(opaque paper doors) of Kohoan.*

fig. 14.10 (right) *The garden path at Kohoan. Notice the fence on the left side and the clipped hedges that serve to create layers of depth within the garden. The small, difficult stepping-stones make the journey seem much longer than it actually is.*

establishing a pure ground that eliminates all the usual signs of casual country living. The urbane participants of the tea ceremony return to a highly cultivated "nature."

The stones of the tea garden often have a more utilitarian purpose than those found in earlier gardens. Cut and uncut stones are used for the paths and walkways, washbasins, and lanterns. All these features developed with the tea garden. Heretofore, the paths of gardens were mostly sand or gravel, but the switch in emphasis to the pathway required stepping stones to protect the moss and guide the way. Selection and placement of these stones was given great attention, for they oriented and paced guests through the garden: If small and difficult to negotiate, they could make a small space seem large; if broad and flat, they might serve as a platform from which to enjoy a particular view. Coupled with the stepping stones, fences or gateways were positioned to emphasize the sense of a transition during the journey to the retreat (Fig. 14.10).

The ritual hand washing required that there be some sort of washbasin along the path. Careful attention was given to this basin, the surrounding drainage area, and the accessory stones that served as resting places for the guests' belongings (Fig. 14.11). Stone lanterns were brought into the garden for the first time with the advent of a nighttime tea ceremony that required low-level lighting. Metal and stone lanterns had been used since ancient days in temples and shrines, but garden lighting was previously provided by temporary wood-and-paper lanterns. Once the use of permanent stone lanterns was established, for utilitarian reasons, they soon became a standard ornament of garden making. They were even added to earlier gardens such as the one on the peninsula in Kinkakuji.

The ornamental use of lanterns is characteristic of garden making in the Edo period. Designs that once had religious, geomantic, or utilitarian functions were simply borrowed in whole or in part to form a primarily visual composition. As garden making began to be practiced by more and more people—made possible by the growth of the middle class, the spread of popular books on

the subject, and the emergence of professional gardeners—the forms became disassociated from their original meanings.

But the tea cult has persisted and thrived, and what the world today usually knows as a "Japanese" garden is either a tea garden or some modification of it. All the essential parts had been developed and employed in the early Edo gardens, which was a culmination of Japanese garden synthesis—one that expressed basic, deep-rooted feelings about nature in a highly refined and stylized way.

NOTES

[1]F. Max Müller, translator and editor, *The Larger Sukhavativyuha, the Smaller Sukhavativyuha and the Amitayurdhyana Sutra* (Sacred Books of the East), vol. 49, Oxford University Press, London, 1894. The description of the Pure Land is in the beginning of the *Smaller Sukhavativyuha.*

[2]A complete history of Japanese Pure land images is found in Joji Okazaki, *Pure Land Buddhist Painting*, Kodansha, Tokyo, 1977. For a contemporary literary description of Heian society, see Edward Seidensticker's translation of Murasaki Shikibu, *The Tale of Genji*, Knopf, New York, 1977.

[3]Akazome Emon (?), *Eiga-monogatari*, early twelfth-century translation by Alexander C. Soper, *The Evolution of Buddhist Architecture in Japan*, Princeton University Press, 1942, pp. 132–133.

[4]Robert T. Paine and Alexander C. Soper, *The Art and Architecture of Japan*, Penguin, Baltimore, 1960, p. 206.

[5]All of the following quotes from the *Sakuteiki* come from Shigemaru Shimoyama's well-rendered translation, Tachibana Toshitsuna, *Sakuteiki: The Book of Garden*, Town and City Planners, Tokyo, 1976. For modern Japanese translations and interpretations, see Tsuyoshi Tamura, *Sakuteiki*, Sagami Shobo, Tokyo, 1964, and Katsuo Saito, *Zukai Sakuteiki*, Giho-do, Tokyo, 1966.

[6]See Bernard Frank, *Kata-Imi et Kata-Tagae: Etude sur les Interdits de Direction à l'époque Heian*, Bulletin de la Maison Franco-Japonaise, Nouvelle Serie, vol. 5, no. 2–4, Tokyo, 1958.

[7]For a complete description of the tea ceremony's history, see A. L. Sadler, *Cha-No-Yu: The Japanese Tea Ceremony*, Tuttle, Tokyo, 1962.

[8]Ishikawa Jozan, in a letter translated by Donald Keene, *World within Walls: Japanese Literature of the Premodern Era, 1600–1867*, Tuttle, Tokyo, 1976 p. 539.

[9]See Ryoichi Fujioka, *Tea Ceremony Utensils*, Arts of Japan, vol. 3, Shibundo/Weatherhill Tokyo, 1973.

fig. 14.11 (above) *Hand-washing area at Katsura Detached Palace. The large stone at the rear serves as the basin, while the guest stands upon the flat white stone in the foreground. The pebbles in between form the drainage area for water runoff. The stones at the sides, as well as the ledge to the right of the basin, are rests for guests' belongings, such as the paper lanterns carried at night.*

part three

The Techniques

chapter fifteen

Principles of Design

ENCLOSURE AND FRAMING

The idea of a separate enclosed area is central to the creation of a Japanese garden; the plans and sections of Part One show that each garden is surrounded by some kind of wall. The enclosure serves to screen out unwanted visual aspects, protect the garden from physical intrusion, and limit the special miniature world created inside. Within its confines, the usual elements of discord and uncertainty are eliminated, ordinary scale is suspended, and an ideal image of landscape is created. This sense of enclosure is particularly important to the Japanese because it is a major characteristic of the Japanese countryside—nothing is unbound and limitless, all is comfortably contained and defined within small valleys and between inland seas. Nothing could be more antithetical to the sense of a Japanese garden than the infinite vistas of Versailles or the unbounded spaces of Le Corbusier.

The widely varying materials used for building fences are discussed in the next chapter , but they are generally of three generic types: The first is a natural-appearing enclosure, usually found in the larger gardens such as Saihoji or Kinkakuji, that consists of large trees or an actual hillside. In practice, trees and earthworks are arranged to conceal the garden wall from view (Figs. 15.1 and 15.2). Gardeners are careful to use evergreens to ensure year-round visual screening. The second type uses the exposed garden wall (either naturally colored as in Ryoanji or whitewashed as in Daisen-in and Shodenji) as a major component of the overall design. Usually found in a Zen temple garden, such a wall may symbolize space extending beyond the actual garden into the background. The third type of enclosure is a mixture of the first two—plant materials are fashioned into artificial shapes and hedges to form the rear wall of the garden, as seen in Entsuji and Kohoan.

Although considerable effort goes into building these barriers, the sense of enclosure never becomes confining or absolute. There is always some visual escape, a sense of promise. Just as the small hillside inside Sambo-in suggests a link with the mountains beyond (Fig. 15.3), so most Japanese gardens characteristically try to offer some visual connection with their surroundings. The principal device for this connection is *shakkei* (borrowed scenery). In Entsuji, for example, distant Mt. Hiei is visually "captured alive"[1] for the overall garden composition and its

An artificial hillside and trees hide the wall.

Planting the trees in a depression places the bulk of the foliage at eye level.

The rear branches are removed, allowing the trees to be planted close together, while the front branches are clipped to form a continuous curtain.

mountain silhouette also helps complete the sense of enclosure (Fig. 9.2). Shodenji, another *shakkei* garden, simply utilizes distant scenery as its final backdrop and limit (Plate 14). A particularly interesting variation of the *shakkei* technique is found at the Joju-in subtemple of Kiyomizu Temple, where a large stone lantern is placed on a nearby hillside. This lantern helps capture and "humanize" the otherwise untouched hillside, which then becomes part of the overall composition and serves as the "back wall" of the garden (Fig. 15.4).

The manner of enclosing the garden is not limited to two dimensions; it includes careful screening of the amount of sky seen above. Overhanging building eaves, large clipped trees, and special "picture windows" located within the garden serve this purpose. Just as space is an element in painting composition, sky is considered a major element in garden composition and must be carefully considered. Too much sky makes the garden unbalanced— too much heaven and not enough earth, too much yang and not enough yin. Unlimited sky also suggests an endless vista that is not in keeping with Japanese feelings about nature.

The "picture window" presents the most obvious connection between gardening and landscape painting: It selects a view and presents it as if it were a painting (Fig. 15.5).

OPPOSITE PAGE:

fig. 15.1 (above) *Obscured from sight by a natural-looking earthen mound and plants, the roof of Sambo-in's garden wall is barely visible during winter.*

fig. 15.2 (below) *Various ways of camouflaging the garden wall with natural materials.*

THIS PAGE:

fig. 15.3 (left) *The artificial hills that screen the Sambo-in garden wall from view also help create the impression that the garden is in the foothills of the mountain beyond.*

fig. 15.4 (upper) *The single lantern in the distance draws the surroundings into the garden. (Edo period garden, Joju-in, Kyoto.)*

fig. 15.5 (lower) *Snow-covered scene from the window of Ginkakuji.*

fig. 15.6 (above) *The wall behind the entryway of Ginkakuji is perforated by a Zen style window that offers a fine view of the garden. (See Fig. 4.7)*

fig. 15.7 (right) *The unhewn structural posts in Katsura Villa heighten the viewer's impression of looking between tree trunks.*

The window is often the light source for a special room known as the *shoin* (study), but it can also be found in a wall whose sole apparent purpose is to serve as a place for a window (Fig. 15.6).

In other gardens, such as Entsuji, Daisen-in, Sambo-in, Shodenji, and Shisendo, the building acts as its own frame. All the sliding doors, which form the outside wall adjacent to the garden, can be removed, whereupon the garden becomes something of a mural surrounding the room (Fig. 6.3). Traditionally, landscape scenes are painted on the inside of sliding doors, so that even people inside a windowless room feel that they are in contact with a landscape. When the doors are removed and the surrounding garden becomes visible, people can feel at one with the landscape. The structural posts help give them the impression of looking between the trunks of trees into the scene and increase their perception of depth in the garden (Fig. 15.7). Both the building floors and eaves help complete the frame, and are considered part of the overall garden composition (Figs. 15.8 and 15.9). Such framed views are often more impressive than the bare garden itself.

PERSPECTIVE AND MINIATURIZATION

There are many parallels between East Asian landscape paintings and the framed garden "pictures." In order to achieve depth, landscape painters utilized parallel plane perspective or the "principle of the three depths."[2] Unlike Western scientific perspective, this system has no ground plane to position elements in space and its verticals do not diminish as they approach a vanishing point. Instead, three major planes are used: foreground, middle distance, and far distance. One's eye must leap from one plane to another across a misty void or a great expanse of sea, as if across an immeasurable distance (Figs. 15.10, 15.11, and 15.12). In the gardens, flat areas of water, moss, or sand act as voids between layers of scenery. The garden's rear hedge can be the middle distance while the borrowed landscape beyond, seen in silhouette, becomes the far-distance plane.

fig. 15.8 (upper) *The large* **sazanka** *(camellia) at Shisendo extends the eave line of the building and helps enclose the garden.*

fig. 15.9 (lower) *View from inside Shisendo is framed by both architectural and garden elements.*

秋林遠岫
辛未孟冬 二□
張學□先生□
張學□大雅

THIS PAGE:

fig. 15.10 (left) Distant Peaks beyond an Autumn Forest, *by Yang Wen-ts'ung (1597–1645), is a clear illustration using three major planes separated by voids to create the illusion of depth (Osaka Museum).*

fig. 15.11 (below, left) *Parallel planes in the composition of Kinkakuji help create the sense of depth. (Photo by Ryusaku Tokuriki.)*

fig. 15.12 (below, right) *The layers of stones seen at Ryoanji similarly illustrate the illusion of depth achieved using parallel plane perspective.*

OPPOSITE PAGE:

fig. 15.13 (top) *Pagodas are usual painting devices for exaggerating the sense of height, as seen here in a scroll painting by Sesshu (1420–1506),* Landscapes of the Four Seasons. *(Collection of Hofu Yamaguchi.)*

fig. 15.14 (center) *The miniature world of Shisendo similarly employs a pagoda to create the illusion of height.*

fig. 15.15 (bottom) *The* manryo (Bladhia lentiginosa) *is a favorite gardening plant that looks like a miniature palm and is often used to create model-like scenery.*

Using parallel plane perspective, the elements of the composition are not restricted in size by any fixed laws. Important features can be magnified to indicate their significance, while distant features that might otherwise be inconspicuous can also be enlarged. Contrarily, elements that would ordinarily appear large can be reduced to suit the needs of the composition. A tree in the foreground will be kept dwarfed lest it obscure the rest of the garden scene. In parallel plane perspective, the size of garden elements can grow either progressively smaller *or* larger as they recede from the main viewpoint, depending on the garden's available space and overall technique. For example, the dwarf pines on the islands in the foreground of Kinkakuji, which are perceived as full size, exaggerate the perception of the pond's breadth (Fig. 15.11). In some mid-size gardens, the smaller elements are placed at the rear, so they appear to have diminished along the lines of "normal" perspective. In a similar way, some garden streams and paths rapidly narrow as they get further away to enhance the illusion of distance.

Within the garden confines, all elements that might serve as reference for normal-scale comparison are eliminated. Instead, the visitor enters a miniature world of intricate detail: A stone becomes a mountain; a clump of moss is a forest; a pond turns into an ocean. More than anything else, the Japanese garden is a model landscape in which the mind can wander through miles of countryside. Pagodas tower above azalea bushes and sand waterfalls cascade down rocks. It is a world of imagination made believable by careful attention to detail and by great skill in manipulating plants (Figs. 15.13, 15.14, and 15.15). Many allied Japanese arts—such as bonsai (miniature plants), tray landscapes, and flower arrangement—not only demonstrate this fascination with minute reproductions of nature but also testify to the skill and patience of the Japanese. Although gardens do not use miniature trees, they do utilize techniques to dwarf normal trees and hold the size of major plants static for centuries.

COMPOSITION

The Japanese garden is a vision of ideal nature, one that intentionally gives an impression of order, harmony, and balance. In order to achieve this ambience, the master garden maker had to walk a delicate path between the casualness and chaos found in everyday nature

on the one hand and the mathematical deadness of a too-regulated order on the other. His ability to succeed depended on a sense of artistic naturalness refined by long hours of study and cultivation, for his garden was an expression of his inner spirit. Masters did not design by a set of formulas but relied instead on insight into their materials. However, certain consistencies in the composition of the gardens do reflect some common underlying design practices.

Both landscape painters and gardeners gave each composition a sense of unity by repeating similar shapes, angles, and patterns throughout the work. Thus mountains, tree branches, and roof slopes may all rise at the same angle, or even have the same silhouette (Figs. 15.16, 15.17, and 15.18). This similarity in contour even applies to the negative shapes—a valley may appear as the mirror image of a mountain (Figs. 15.19 and 15.20). Similar forms and patterns echoing throughout the composition can be seen as the working of a great universal design, one in which the creations of people are in harmony with nature.

The connection between different garden elements is often made by a careful interlocking of parts. One material is shaped as the mirror opposite of another, forming a kind of jigsaw puzzle joint favored throughout the gardens (Figs. 15.19, 15.20, and 15.21). This close integration and accommodation of different materials is essential in creating the garden's spirit of harmony.

Those garden elements not directly joined to each other are, of course, separated by space. In East Asian landscape art, space is both poignant with meaning and a crucial factor in the design. As the opposite of form, it plays an equal role in creation—representing the inexpressible, the mysterious, the deep. Thus the quality and shape of space is given at least as much concern as form, for "it is the void of a vessel that gives it its usefulness." The relation of space to composition was put succinctly by a Chinese painting master: "Whenever one paints landscapes, one must pay attention to proper dividing and combining; the spacing is the main principle. There is the spacing of the whole composition and the spacing of the parts of the picture. If one understands this, one has grasped more than half of the principles of painting."[3] The same can be said about the design of a garden, except that a garden has both real three-dimensional space—the "thin air" between

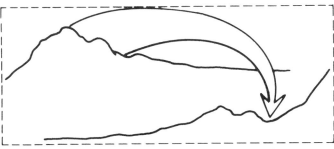

objects and the sky above—and symbolic space—the "blank" planes of wall and ground covering that function like the unpainted areas of the landscape paintings. It is the shape of these spaces that creates enough tension to hold the work together and give it cohesiveness. Too much space and the work flies apart; too little and it looks cramped and cluttered.

The space within the garden is not evenly divided down the middle by either a central axis or a prominent feature. Ever since the breakdown of Chinese patterned symmetric arrangements in the Heian period, overall plans and individual groupings of Japanese gardens have been laid out asymmetrically. Asymmetric designs establish a sense of visual balance through a proportioning of masses and distances so that $M \times D = C$. M is the psychological weight or mass of an object. D is the distance between it and the real or imaginary fulcrum, and C remains constant[4] (Fig. 15.24). This formula, of course, depends on the input of subjective values, but it indicates the consistency of asymmetric balance.

The scalene triangle is both an asymmetric and a stable-looking balanced form. Partially for these reasons, it is a favorite shape for stones and other groupings (Fig. 15.25). The major stone forms the off-center apex of the triangle, and two or more stones make up the base of the entire composition. Garden making texts,[5] which became popular in Japan during the Edo period, offered many suggestions for standardized patterns and "golden formulas" designating proper ratios for a balanced composition; today such texts recommend interlocking scalene triangles as the basis for the design of the garden plan and elevations. The 3:5:7 combination has been the most popular formula since Edo gardens, used for such factors as the length of the sides of triangles, proportions of height, and number of elements in groupings (Figure 8.4 and Plate 14).

Most other aspects of the design are similarly asymmetric. The appropriate ratios of light and dark, form and space, horizontals and verticals, and even yin and yang features of the landscape were never exactly equal to each other. They too were consciously balanced in an asymmetric way.

NOTES

[1] This translation of *shakkei* is suggested by Teiji Itoh, *Space and Illusion in the Japanese Garden*, Weatherhill/Tankosha, Tokyo, 1973.

[2] George Rowley, *Principles of Chinese Painting*, Princeton University Press, 1959, pp. 64–65.

[3] Tung Ch'i-ch'ang, *Hua-yen (Ming Dynasty)*, translated by George Rowley, ibid, pp. 56–57.

[4] This formula is suggested in Kunio Shimode, ed., *Nihon no Toshikukan (Japanese Urban Space)*, Shokokusha, Tokyo, 1969, p. 36.

[5] The most important was the *Tsukiyama Teizoden*. The first part was written in 1735 by Kitamura Enkin, and the second part was added in 1828 by Akizato Rito. See Keiji Uehara, ed., Kajima Shoten, Tokyo, 1960, for a recent edition.

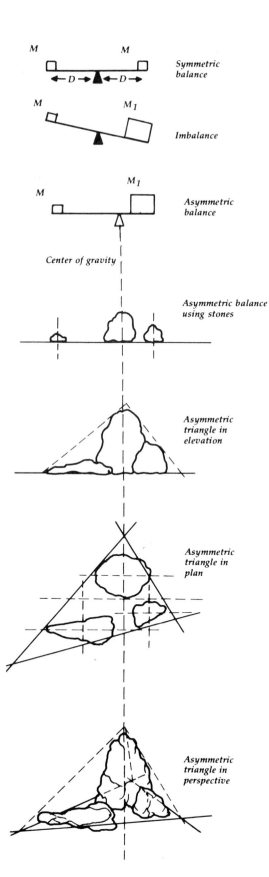

M   M

Symmetric
balance

←D→←D→

M M_1

Imbalance

M_1

M

Asymmetric
balance

Center of gravity

Asymmetric balance
using stones

Asymmetric
triangle in
elevation

Asymmetric
triangle in
plan

Asymmetric
triangle in
perspective

OPPOSITE PAGE:

fig. 15.22 (upper)   *The foundation stone at the base of this basin at Kohoan is integrated with the cut-stone curb. The plant is trained to act as a continuation of the basin's top plane, thereby connecting dissimilar materials with a similar form.*

fig. 15.23 (lower)   *The bamboo fence at Ginkakuji is carefully constructed to accommodate the living tree trunk.*

THIS PAGE:

fig. 15.24 (left)   *Asymmetric balance and triangular composition in stone groupings.*

fig. 15.25 (above)   *Triangular stone composition at Daisen-in.*

chapter sixteen

Construction Details

The photos of this chapter are meant to serve as a visual appendix covering the construction of some principal garden components: bridges and paths, fences and gates, and water features. A section on plant maintenance lists the principal varieties found in the gardens along with notes concerning their planting and care.

BRIDGES AND PATHS

Elaborate high-arched Chinese style bridges, once a main feature in Heian period gardens, are not found in any of the gardens surveyed. Bridges made from uncut stones are most common, followed by those made from cut stone and wood.

The early garden paths were made of gravel or sand. With the advent of the tea garden, path construction became a highly developed art employing cut or uncut stones, either separately or together.

OPPOSITE PAGE:

fig. 16.1 (left) *This stone bridge at Saihoji looks natural and is functional as well.*

fig. 16.2 (right, top) *A tree root reinforced with sticks forms another bridge at Saihoji.*

fig. 16.3 (right, center) *The pond in Ginkakuji is drained once every ten years to remove silt from the bottom. Here the details of stone placement are clearly revealed.*

fig. 16.4 (right, bottom) *Another bridge at Ginkakuji. Large stones, resembling pylons, are placed at the four corners where the span meets the shoreline. Notice also the foundation work.*

THIS PAGE:

fig. 16.5 (left, above) *The same bridge, with the pond at its usual level.*

fig. 16.6 (left, below) *At Daisen-in the bridge construction is very similar to that of Ginkakuji, but here it is merely symbolic.*

fig. 16.7 (right, above) *Another symbolic bridge at Kohoan.*

THIS PAGE:

fig. 16.8 (left, above) *The elegant cut-stone bridge at Kohoan is considered one of the finest in the city. Here the pylons at the four corners have been reduced in height but are still present. It is interesting to note that such sophistication was not considered contrary to the objective of creating a simple, humble hermitage.*

fig. 16.9 (right, above) *The height of this bridge at Sambo-in would permit boats to pass underneath. Large sticks, placed horizontally across the wooden frame, are covered with earth and moss.*

fig. 16.10 (right, below) *A clear-span wooden bridge in the rear tea garden of Sambo-in.*

OPPOSITE PAGE:

fig. 16.11 (top, right) *Stepping stones at Kohoan.*

fig. 16.12 (top, left) *Natural stepping stones placed to form a staircase at Katsura Imperial Villa.*

fig. 16.13 (center, left) *Cut stones and snow-covered moss at the entrance to Daisen-in.*

fig. 16.14 (center, right) *Entrance pathway to Kohoan. The top corner stone suggests the change in direction.*

fig. 16.15 (bottom, left) *Cut stones used in the foundation line, natural stepping stones, moss and gravel meet at a single point in Kohoan.*

fig. 16.16 (bottom, right) *A tree root is carefully integrated with the modern concrete walk at Saihoji. Notice also the drain gutter, which begins above the left side of the root, passes beneath it, and continues on to the right.*

FENCES AND GATES

There are innumerable ways of combining earth, stone, and living or dead plant material to form fences and gates. These photos illustrate the major types and some particularly noteworthy details.

THIS PAGE:

fig. 16.17 (right, top) *The entrance to Ginkakuji, containing a mixture of the most common fencing materials. The eroding section of the wall reveals the numerous layers of different earth mixtures used in construction.*

fig. 16.18 (above) *The interior core of this earthen wall at Daitokuji contains fragments of old roof tiles.*

fig. 16.19 (right, center) *This well-maintained wall at Saihoji is interrupted so that the stream can enter the garden.*

fig. 16.20 (right, bottom) *The standard temple gateway at Saihoji has a tiled roof.*

OPPOSITE PAGE:

fig. 16.21 (top) *This inner gateway at Kinkakuji is typical of the more rustic style. Moss and ferns have started growing in the thatched roof. (See also Ch. 10.)*

fig. 16.22 (right, center) *Construction details of a similar gateway in Nishihonganji temple illustrated in an old gardening text.*

fig. 16.23 (left, bottom) *This wooden gateway at Kohoan, like all the other features of the garden, is highly refined.*

fig. 16.24 (right, bottom) *This bamboo fence (2 feet high) at Kohoan is placed atop an earthen mound. Its presence is entirely symbolic.*

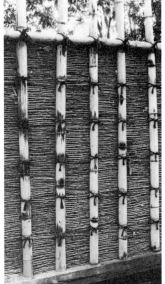

fig. 16.25 (top, left) *Bamboo fence mixed with a long-leaf podocarp hedge in Daitokuji Temple, near Kohoan.*

fig. 16.26 (top, center) *Yet another use of bamboo—as a casement for woven branches at Katsura. (See Note 1, Ch. 11.)*

fig. 16.27 (top, right) *The same motif as Fig. 16.26, but used in a more casual way at Shisendo.*

fig. 16.28 (lower, right) *Detail of the bamboo dovetailing with the wooden frame of the Shisendo entrance gate. (See Fig. 10.6.)*

fig. 16.29 (lower, left) *Of all the hedges used as fences (see Figs. 11.6 and 9.6), this one at Shisendo is the most complex.*

WATER FEATURES

Water is used in half the gardens surveyed. By far the most important feature is the large central pond. Streams have relatively little visual impact. They are narrow, near the boundaries of the garden, and usually feed the waterfalls that pour into the pond. The handling of rainwater runoff in the gardens is surprisingly open and imaginative. Overall pond design and waterfalls are illustrated in the individual garden chapters; the photos here show details of shore construction, drainage devices, and the special features of Shisendo.

fig. 16.30 (above, left) *The pond edge at Ginkakuji after draining. The change in coloration shows the normal waterline.*

fig. 16.31 (above, right) *Pond edge at Sambo-in. Notice the dovetailed joint between the shore stone and the foundation stone.*

fig. 16.32 (left) *Island in the Kinkakuji pond.*

fig. 16.33 (left, upper) *Wooden poles used to stabilize the shore at Saihoji.*

fig. 16.34 (left, lower) *Similar wood-and-pebble construction used along the shore of the pond in front of the Ryoanji rock garden.*

fig. 16.35 (right, top) *Traditionally, structures did not have roof-mounted rain gutters but used instead gravel troughs on the ground under the eaves to collect and control rainwater runoff. Here at Sambo-in the trough is used as a permanent stream that feeds the tea garden waterfall.*

fig. 16.36 (right, bottom) *The gravel trough at Ginkakuji feeds directly into the pond seen in the upper part of the picture.*

fig. 16.37 (left, upper)   *A cut-stone gutter runs
directly through the entrance path of Kohoan.
Something that would ordinarily be concealed or
camouflaged is instead openly displayed.*

fig. 16.38 (left, lower)   *Roof-mounted gutters
made of split bamboo are used on later
buildings—for example, here in Shisendo. The
drainpipes are also bamboo.*

fig. 16.39 (right, top)   *The hedge at Shisendo is
clipped to reveal the presence of a small stream.*

fig. 16.40 (right, bottom)   *Detail of Fig. 16.39.*

fig. 16.41 The **shishi-odoshi** (deer-frightening noisemaker) at Shisendo. Patterned after noisemakers used in the country to protect crops, it becomes here an acoustic ornament that makes a pleasant clacking sound every half minute.

PLANT MAINTENANCE

The traditional Japanese garden is not a botanical garden used to exhibit a large number of unusual plants. Indeed, not many varieties are used, and those used are common plants, well adapted to the environment. But the time and energy that goes into maintaining these plants in ideal condition is extraordinary.

fig. 16.42 (left) *Pruning the dwarf pine in Katsura Imperial Villa. The entire tree is thinned by hand, needle by needle.*

fig. 16.43 (above) *Cleaning up after clipping the hedges.*

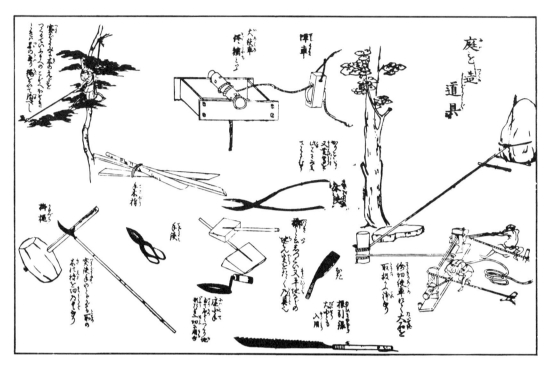

庭造道具

OPPOSITE PAGE:

fig. 16.44 (top) *Illustration of Edo period gardening tools and techniques from the Tsukiyama Teizoden. (See Note 5, Ch. 15.)*

fig. 16.45 (below, left) *Training a young pine at Ginkakuji to lean away from the pavilion.*

fig. 16.46 (below, right) *Branches that overhang the pond are especially desirable, and supports—such as this one at Ginkakuji—are often necessary.*

THIS PAGE:

fig. 16.47 (top, left) *An elaborately trained pine at the entrance of Daisen-in. The one found in Kinkakuji is shaped to resemble a ship.*

fig. 16.48 (below, left) *An arbor for wisteria in Saihoji.*

fig. 16.49 (top, right) *At the turn of the seventeenth century, sago palms were brought from southern locales and used in Kyoto gardens. Straw wrappings protect them from the winter cold, as shown here at Katsura. Similar palms are used in Sambo-in.*

fig. 16.50 (below, right) *Moss beds at Sambo-in are shaped to resemble sake cups and gourds. (See Fig. 7.6.)*

Fig. 16.51 *Table of Selected Plant Materials*[1]

Botanical Name	Japanese Name	English Name	Height
Evergreen trees			
Abies firma	Momi	Japanese fir	30 m
Castanopsis cuspidate	Shii	Japanese chinquapin	30 m
Chamaecyparis obtusa	Hinoki	Hinoki cypress	15–20 m
Chamaecyparis pisifera	Sawara	Sawara cypress	5–10 m
Cinnamomum camphora	Kusu	Camphor tree	30 m
Cleyera japonica	Sakaki		10 m
Cryptomeria japonica	Sugi	Cryptomeria	15–50 m
Cycas revoluta	Sotetsu	Sago palm	3–4 m
Daphniphyllum macropodum	Yuzuriha		15 m
Dendropanax trifidus	Kakuremino		8 m
Distylium racemosum	Isunoki	Isu tree	10–15 m
Ilex integra	Mochinoki		10 m
Ilex latifolia	Tarayo	Lusterleaf holly	15 m
Ilex rotunda	Kuroganemochi		10–15 m
Illicium religiosum	Shikimi	Japanese anise tree	3–6 m
Osmanthus fragrans	Mokusei	Sweet osmanthus	6 m
Osmanthus ilicifolius	Hiirage	Holly osmanthus	4–8 m
Pinus densiflora	Akamatsu	Japanese red pine	20 m
Pinus thunbergii	Kuromatsu	Japanese black pine	20 m
Podocarpus chinensis	Rakanmaki		5–6 m
Quercus glauca	Arakashi	Blue Japanese oak	10–20 m
Quercus phillyraeoides	Ubamegashi		15 m

Habitat	Location	Remarks
Moist clay soil, shady or sunny site, big and deep root, lives 100–150 years	G, S	Elipsoid tree form
Fertile soil, fast-growing, easy to clip and transplant	Sam, Ko	
Moist or dry soil, hard to transplant	All but Sho	Elipsoid tree form
Sunny site, short life, easy to clip	K, G	
Any soil, fast-growing, difficult to transplant, pollution-resistant	K, G, Ko	
Fertile soil, fast-growing	S, G, K, Sam, Shi, Ko	Used in shrines
Any soil, use care in transplanting (pollution sensitive)	S, D, G, Sam, E, Ko	Connifer, elipsoid tree form
Sunny and dry site, easy to transplant	Sam	
Shady site, slow-growing, difficult to transplant, resistant to sea breeze	S, G, Ko	
Shady site, slow-growing, difficult to transplant, easy to prune	K	Used in tea gardens and shrines
Any soil, shady site, easy to clip, resistant to sea breeze	G, Ko	Flowers in April–May
Shady site, full-size tree likes sun	K, G, Sam	Used in shrines
Shady site, slow-growing, easy to transplant	G, D, Ko	Sutras written on broad leaves
Shady site, slow-growing, easy to transplant, resistant to sea breeze	K, G, Sam	Fragrant, small white flowers
Shady and moist site, slow-growing, resistant to clipping	S, Sam	
Fast-growing, easy to prune	S	Flowers in September, fragrant tree
Shady and moist site, fast-growing, easy to transplant, resistant to pruning and pollution	Shi, Sam, Ko	
Dry and nonfertile soil, transplanting possible, not resistant to pruning	S, K, G, Sam, Shi, Ko	Picturesque tree form
Dry and nonfertile soil, transplanting possible, not resistant to pruning	S, K, G, Sam, D	Picturesque tree form
Slow-growing, easy to transplant, resistant to pruning and sea breeze	S, G, Shi, E, D	
Sunny and fertile site, fast-growing, pruning easy	All but Sho	March foliage turns from green to red
Shady site, slow-growing, pruning easy, resistant to pollution and dry soil, difficult to transplant	G, Sam, D	

Key:
S = Saihoji
K = Kinkakuji
G = Ginkakuji
D = Daisen-in
E = Entsuji
Sam = Sambo-in
Shi = Shisendo
Sho = Shodenji
Ko = Kohoan

fig. 16.51 *Table of Selected Plant Materials*[1] *(Cont.)*

Botanical Name	Japanese Name	English Name	Height
Deciduous trees			
Acer palmatum	*Momiji*	Japanese maple	5–10 m
Diospyros kaki	*Kaki*	Japanese persimmon	5–15 m
Lagerstroemia indica	*Sarusuberi*	Crape myrtle	5–10 m
Prunus denarium var. spontanea	*Yamazakura*	Mountain cherry	5–10 m
Quercus acutissima	*Kunugi*	Sawtooth oak	8–18 m
Quercus serrata	*Konara*		15 m
Deciduous bushes			
Ilex serata var. sieboldii	*Umemodoki*	Japanese winter berry	2–5 m
Lespedeza bicolor var. japonica	*Hagi*	Bush clover	1–2 m
Rhododendron dilatatum	*Mitsubatsutsuji*	Azalea	1–2 m
Rhododendron linearifolium var. macrosepalum	*Mochitsutsuji*	Big sepal azalea	1–2 m
Rhododendron obtusum var. Kaempferi	*Yamatsutsuji*	Torch azalea	2–3 m
Spiraea thunbergii	*Yukiyanagi*		1–1.5 m
Evergreen bushes			
Aucuba japonica	*Aoki*	Japanese aucuba	3 m
Bladhia lentiginosa	*Manryo*		.6–1 m
Camellia japonica	*Yamatsubaki*	Common camellia	5–10 m
Camellia japonica var. hortensis	*Tsubaki*	Japanese camellia	5–10 m
Camellia sasanqua	*Sazanka*	Sasanqua camellia	3 m
Eurya japonica	*Hisakaki*		5 m

Habitat	Location	Remarks
Hardy, slow-growing, shapes well	S, K, G, Sam, E, Shi, Ko	Leaves have good fall color
Sunny site, slow-growing, difficult to transplant, resistant to clipping	Shi	Orange-colored fruit
Any soil, sunny site, easy to prune	S, G, Ko	Pinkish flowers in July–Sept.
Moist and drained soil, not resistant to pruning	S, K	Pink-and-white flowers in April
Any soil, deep root, not resistant to pruning	S	Foliage in November turns from brown to yellow
Shady site, resistant to dry soil	K, G	
Fertile soil, slow-growing, easy to transplant	S, K, G, Shi	Fruit turns red in October–November
Fertile soil, shady site, fast-growing, deep root, easy to transplant	K, Shi	Pale purple-and-white flower in October
Half sunny and half shady site, slow-growing, easy to transplant, resistant to pruning	S, K, Ko	Earliest azalea to flower
Half sunny and half shady, slow-growing, easy to transplant, resistant to pruning	S, K, G	Pink flowers in April–May
Half sunny and half shady, slow-growing, easy to transplant, resistant to pruning	K, Shi	Bright red flowers in May
Half sunny and half shady site, fast-growing	Shi	Small white flowers in March–April
Moist soil, not resistant to pruning	S, K, G, Sam, Shi, D	Red fruit
Moist and fertile soil, half shady site, not resistant to pruning	S, K, Sam, D, Ko	Red to pale yellow fruit in October (miniature palm)
Shady site, slow-growing, easy to clip and transplant, pollution resistant	All but Sho	Multicolored flowers, February–Arpil
Shady site, slow-growing, easy to clip and transplant, pollution resistant	All but Sho	Multicolored flowers February–April
Fertile soil, sunny site, easy to prune	All but K	White, pink, and red flowers in October
Slow-growing, resistant to sea breeze	S, K, Sam, Sho	Hedge used in tea gardens

Key:
S = Saihoji
K = Kinkakuji
G = Ginkakuji
D = Daisen-in
E = Entsuji
Sam = Sambo-in
Shi = Shisendo
Sho = Shodenji
Ko = Kohoan

fig. 16.51 *Table of Selected Plant Materials*[1] *(Cont.)*

Botanical Name	Japanese Name	English Name	Height
Gardenia jasminoides	*Kuchinashi*	Cape jasmine	2 m
Ilex crenata	*Inutsuge*	Japanese holly	2–6 m
Ligustrum japonicum	*Nezuminochi*	Japanese privet	3–4 m
Nandina domestica	*Nanten*	Heavenly bamboo	1–2 m
Photinia glabra	*Kanamemochi*	Japanese photinia	5 m
Pieris japonica	*Asebi*	Japanese andromeda	6–10 m
Rhododendron jateritium	*Satsuki*	Satsuki azalea	.5–1 m
Rhododendron indicum	*Hiradotsutsuji*	Azalea	1–3 m
Rhododendron obtusum	*Kirishimatsutsuji*	Azalea	1–3 m
Serissa foetida	*Hakuchoge*	Japanese serrisa	.6–1 m
Ternstroemia gymnanthera	*Mokkoku*		5–15 m
Thea sinesis	*Cha*	Tea	1–2 m
Vaccinium bracteatum	*Shashanpo*		1–5 m

NOTES

Some basic construction information in English is given in: David Engel, *Japanese Gardens for Today*, Tuttle, Tokyo, 1959; Isamu Kashikie, *The ABC of Japanese Gardening*, Japan Publications Trading Co., Tokyo, 1963; Samuel Newsom, *A Japanese Garden Manual for Westerners*, Tokyo News Service, 1965.

[1]Plants that appear only in a single garden are omitted unless they play a major role in that garden's design. Classification, habitat, and remarks are based on Ryo Iishima and Toshihibo Anbiru, *Niwaki to Ryokkaju, (Garden Trees and Forestration)*, vols. 1 and 2. Seibundo, Tokyo, 1973. The most comprehensive list of Japanese garden plant materials, including modern uses, is found in Japanese in Kinsaku Nakane, *Niwa Meien no Kansho to Sakutei (Fine Garden Appreciation and Construction)*, Hoikusha, Osaka, 1973, pp. 207–218.

Habitat	Location	Remarks
Any soil	S, K, D, Ko	White, fragrant flowers in June
Moist soil, easy to transplant and clip	S, G, Sam	Hedge
Shady site, fast-growing; easy to transplant, resistant to sea breeze and pollution	S, K, G, Sam, Shi	Flowers in June
Sunny and moist site	S, Sam, Sho, Shi, D, Ko	White flowers in June red-and-white fruit in October
Partly sunny site, fast-growing, slightly difficult to transplant, pollution-resistant	All but Sho, E	Pink-and-white flowers in May–June
Fertile soil, easy to transplant, easy to prune	S, K, G, Sam, Ko	White flowers in April–May
Any soil, shady site, easy to transplant, easy to prune	All	Red-and-purple flowers in June–August (common hedge)
Any soil, shady site, easy to transplant, easy to prune	K	Multicolored flowers
Any soil, shady site, slow-growing, easy to prune	S, K	Multicolored flowers in May
Any soil, easy to prune	S, Ko	White-and-light-purple flowers in June
Sunny and fertile site, easy to transplant	S, G, Sam, Shi, Ko	Yellow-and-white flowers in June
Both sunny and shady sites, slow-growing, deep root, difficult to transplant	S, K, G, Sho, Shi, Ko	White flowers with slight fragrance in October–November
Sunny site, easy to prune, slightly difficult to transplant	S, K, G, Sam, Shi, Ko	White flowers in June–July

Key:
  S = Saihoji
  K = Kinkakuji
  G = Ginkakuji
  D = Daisen-in
  E = Entsuji
Sam = Sambo-in
Shi = Shisendo
Sho = Shodenji
Ko = Kohoan

Bibliography

BOOKS IN WESTERN LANGUAGES

Austin, Robert, Dana Levy, and Koichiro Ueda: *Bamboo*, Weatherhill, New York, 1977.

Bary, Wm. T. de, ed.: *Sources of Japanese Tradition, vol. 1*, Columbia, New York, 1958.

Beardsley, Richard, John W. Hale, and Robert E. Ward: *Village Japan*, Chicago, University of Chicago Press, 1972.

Blacker, Carmen: *The Catalpa Bow: A Study of Shamanistic Practices in Japan*, G. Allen, London, 1975.

Boyd, Andrew: *Chinese Architecture 1500 B.C.–A.D. 1911*, Alec Tiranti, London, 1962.

Capra, Fritjof: *The Tao of Physics*, Bantam, New York, 1977.

Conder, Josiah: *Landscape Gardening of Japan*, 1893, Dover reprint, New York, 1963.

Czaja, Michael: *Gods of Myth and Stone: Phallicism in Japanese Folk Religion*, Weatherhill, Tokyo, 1974.

Dumoulin, Heinrich S. J.: *A History of Zen Buddhism*, Beacon Press, Boston, 1963.

Eitel, E. J.: *Fen-shui; Principles of the Natural Science of the Chinese*, Lane, Crawford, Hong Kong, 1872.

Engel, David: *Japanese Gardens for Today*, Tuttle, Tokyo, 1959.

Engel, Heinrich: *The Japanese House: A Tradition for Contemporary Architecture*, Tuttle, Vermont, 1964.

Fenollosa, Ernest F.: *Epochs of Chinese and Japanese Art, vol. 1*, Dover, New York, 1963.

Feuchtwang, Stephan D. R.: *An Anthropological Analysis of Chinese Geomancy*, Editions Vithagna, Vientiane, 1974.

Frank, Bernard: *Kata-Imi et Kata-Tagae: Etude sur les Interdits de Direction à l'époque Heian*, Bulletin de la Maison Franco-Japonaise, Nouvelle Serie, vol. 5, no. 2–4, Tokyo, 1958.

Fujioka, Ryoichi: *Tea Ceremony Utensils*, Arts of Japan, vol. 4, Shibundo/Weatherhill, Tokyo, 1973.

Fukuyama, Toshio: *Heian Temples: Byodo-in and Chusoji*, Weatherhill/Heibonsha, Tokyo, 1976.

Fung, Yu-Lan, ed. by Derk Bodde: *A Short History of Chinese Philosophy*, Macmillan, New York, 1958.

Gouverneur, Mosher: *Kyoto: A Contemplative-Guide*, Tuttle, Tokyo, 1964.

Hayakawa, Masao: *The Garden Art of Japan*, Weatherhill/Heibonsha, Tokyo, 1965.

Hisamatsu, Shin'ichi: *Zen and the Fine Arts*, Kodansha International, Tokyo, 1965.

Iguchi, Kaisen: *Tea Ceremony*, Hoikusha, Tokyo, 1976.

Inn, Henry: *Chinese Homes and Gardens*, Hastings House, New York, 1950.

Itoh, Teiji: *The Japanese Garden*, Yale, New Haven, 1972.

————: *Space and Illusion in the Japanese Garden*, Weatherhill/Tankosha, Tokyo, 1965.

Kageyama, Haruiki: *The Arts of Shinto*, Arts of Japan, vol. 4, Shibundo/Weatherhill, Tokyo, 1973.

Kashikie, Isamu: *The ABC of Japanese Gardening*, Japan Publishing Trading Co., Tokyo, 1963.

Keene, Donald: *World within Walls: Japanese Literature of the Premodern Era, 1600–1867*, Tuttle, Tokyo, 1976.

Kidder, J. E.: *Japan Before Buddhism*, Thames & Hudson, London, 1959.

Kuck, Loraine: *The World of the Japanese Garden*, Walker/Weatherhill, Tokyo, 1968.

Lethaby, William R.: *Architecture, Mysticism and Myth*, George Braziller, New York, 1975.

Masuda, Tomoya: *Living Architecture: Japanese*, Grosset & Dunlap, New York, 1970.

Mishima, Yukio, translated by Ivan Morris: *The Temple of the Golden Pavilion*, Tuttle, Tokyo, 1959.

Mori, Osamu: *Typical Japanese Gardens*, Shibata/Japan Publications, Tokyo, 1962.

Morse, Edward: *Japanese Homes and Their Surroundings*, Tuttle, Tokyo (1888) 1972.

Nakane, Kinsaku: *Kyoto Gardens*, Hoikusha, Osaka, 1967.

Needham, Joseph: *Science and Civilization in China, vols. 2, 3, 4*, Cambridge University Press, 1959–1964.

Newsom, Samuel: *A Japanese Garden Manual for Westerners*, Tokyo News Service, 1965.

Okazaki, Joji, translated by Elizabeth ten Grotenhuis: *Pure Land Buddhist Painting*, Kodansha, Tokyo, 1977.

Okakura, Kakuzo: *The Book of Tea*, Dover, New York, (1906) 1956.

Ono, Sokyo: *Shinto: The Kami Way*, Tuttle, Tokyo, 1962.

Paine, Robert T., and Alexander C. Soper: *The Art and Architecture of Japan*, Penguin, Baltimore, 1960.

Rambach, Pierre and Susanne: *Le Livre Secret des Jardins Japonais*, Albert Skira, Geneva, 1973.

Rawson, Philip, and Laszlo Legeza: *Tao: The Chinese Philosophy of Time and Change*, Thames and Hudson, London, 1973.

Rowley, George: *Principles of Chinese Painting*, Princeton University Press, Princeton, N.J., 1959.

Sadler, A. L.: *Cha-No-Yu: The Japanese Tea Ceremony*, Tuttle, Tokyo, 1962.

Sansom, G. B.: *Japan: A Short Cultural History*, Tuttle, Tokyo (1931), 1976.

Seckel, Dietrick: *The Art of Buddhism*, Crown Publishers, New York, 1963.

Seidensticker, Edward, translator: *The Tale of Genji*, by Murasaki Shikibu, Knopf, New York, 1977.

Sekida, Katsuki: *Two Zen Classics: Mumonkan and Hekiganroku*, Weatherhill, Tokyo, 1977.

Shimoyama, Shigemaru, translator: *Sakuteiki: The Book of Garden* by Toshitsuna Tachibana, Town and City Planners, Tokyo, 1976.

Soper, Alexander C.: *The Evolution of Buddhist Architecture in Japan*, Princeton University Press, 1942.

Stein, Rolf: *Jardin en miniature d'Extrême Orient,"* Bulletin de l'Ecole Française d'Extrême Orient, vol. 42, Hanoi, 1943.

Tanaka, Ichimatsu: *Japanese Ink Painting: Shubun to Sesshu*, Weatherhill/Heibonsha, Tokyo, 1972.

Tange, Kenzo, and Walter Gropius: *Katsura: Tradition and Creation in Japanese Architecture*, Yale, New Haven, 1960.

Tange, Kenzo: *Ise Prototype of Japanese Architecture*, M.I.T., Boston, 1962.

Watanabe, Yasutada: *Shinto Art: Ise and Izumo Shrines*, Weatherhill/Heibonsha, Tokyo, 1974.

Wheatley, Paul: *The Pivot of the Four Corners*, Edinburgh University Press, 1971.

Yoon, Hong-key: *Geomantic Relationships between Culture and Nature in Korea*, Orient Cultural Service, Taipei, 1976.

Yoshimura, Yuji, and Giovanna M. Halford: *The Japanese Art of Miniature Trees and Landscapes*, Tuttle, Tokyo, 1957.

BOOKS IN JAPANESE

Domon, Ken, and Seishi Yamaguchi: *Nihon no Tera: Saihoji, Ryoanji (Japanese Temples: Saihoji, Ryoanji)*, Bijitsu Shuppansha, Tokyo, 1959.

Iishima, Ryo, and Toshihibo Anbiru: *Niwaki to Ryokkaju (Garden Trees and Forestration)*, vols. 1 and 2, Seibundo, Tokyo, 1973.

Mori, Osamu: *Nippon no Niwa (Japanese Gardens)*, with English summary, Asahi Shimbun Shuppansha, Tokyo, 1960.

Nakane, Kinsaku: *Niwa Meien no Kansho to Sakutei (Fine Garden Appreciation and Construction)*, Hoikusha, Osaka, 1973.

Saito, Katsuo: *Zukai Sakuteiki (Pictorial Explanation of Sakuteiki)*, Giho-do, Tokyo, 1966.

Sekino, Masaru, ed.: *Nihon no Bijitsu 2, No. 153: Kinkaku to Ginkaku (Arts of Japan, vol. 2, Kinkaku and Ginkaku)*, Shibundo, Tokyo, 1979.

Shigemori, Mirei: *Nihon Teien Shi Zukan (Illustrated History of Japanese Gardens)*, 26 vols., Yukosha, Tokyo, 1936–1939.

Shimode, Kunio, ed.: *Nihon no Toshikukan (Japanese Urban Space)*, Shokokusha, Tokyo, 1969.

Tomura, Tsuyoshi: *Sakuteiki*, Sagami Shobo, Tokyo, 1964.

Uehara, Keiji, ed.: *Tsukiyama Teizoden (A Tradition of Garden Making)*, Kajima Shoten, Tokyo, 1960.

Yoshinaga, Yoshinobu: *Nihon no Teien (Japanese Traditional Gardens)*, English and Japanese, Shokokusha, Tokyo, 1962.

Index